• HALSGROVE DISCOVER SERIES ➤

THE SURREY HILLS

BEATA MOORE

HALSGROVE

First published in Great Britain in 2014

Copyright © Beata Moore 2014

British Library Cataloguing-in-Publication Data
A CIP record for this title is available from the British Library

ISBN 978 0 85704 224 8

HALSGROVE
Halsgrove House,
Ryelands Business Park,
Bagley Road, Wellington, Somerset TA21 9PZ
Tel: 01823 653777   Fax: 01823 216796
email: sales@halsgrove.com

Part of the Halsgrove group of companies
Information on all Halsgrove titles is available at:
www.halsgrove.com

Printed in China by Everbest Printing Co Ltd

" As always, with love, to John, my husband"

CONTENTS

	Introduction	5
Chapter 1	**Around Farnham**	23
Chapter 2	**Around Guildford**	43
Chapter 3	**Around Dorking**	79
Chapter 4	**Around Reigate**	111
	Annex	139

Introduction

THE SURREY HILLS IS A nationally important Area of Outstanding Natural Beauty (AONB) covering a quarter of the county of Surrey. Its boundary stretches from Farnham in the west to Oxted in the east and extends to Haslemere all the way in the south. Since 1958, the Surrey Hills is a protected landscape, having an equal landscape status and protection to a National Park. Part of the area is owned and managed by the National Trust, the Woodland Trust and Surrey Wildlife Trust. The Surrey Hills Board is a body protecting and promoting this area. The main founding members of the Board are: Guildford Borough Council, Mole Valley District Council, Reigate and Banstead Borough Council, Tandridge District Council, Surrey County Council, Waverely Borough Council and Natural England. The very diverse landscapes of the Surrey Hills cover wooded areas (almost 40%), heathland (18%), chalk grass, farmlands, ponds, rivers and parklands. The area is very popular with visitors; an extensive network of foot paths, bridleways and cycle routes takes walkers and cyclists to remote villages, isolated hamlets and beauty spots like Leith Hill, Box Hill, Holmbury Hill and the Devil's Punch Bowl. The Surrey Hills inspired many artists and writers: Sir Edwin Lutyens, Gertrude Jekyll, Sir Arthur Conan Doyle, Alfred, Lord Tennyson, Jane Austen, George Elliot and many more. The bustling market towns of Dorking, Farnham, Guildford, Reigate, Haslemere and Cranleigh offer cobbled streets, twisting lanes, centuries-old buildings and

Beech wood in autumn in Abinger Roughs.

Opposite: Sunrise at Newlands Corner.

5

Polesden Lacey, Great Bookham.

Leith Hill Tower at Leith Hill.

castles as well as a variety of shops, restaurants and tea rooms in modern but also historic timber-framed buildings. There are also plenty of tiny hamlets and villages with Norman and medieval churches, extensive village greens, characteristic old inns, pubs and blacksmiths. In some of the villages there are hammer or mill ponds, the sign of the industrial past of the area. Many houses in the area are in a characteristic "Surrey style" introduced here by the Arts and Crafts movement. They are built from local materials, bricks and clay tiles, sandstone, flint and timber. Winding country lanes with high banks enclosed by ancient beech and oak as well as the old signs and milestones reinforce the rural character of the bygone era. The very narrow, sometimes single track lanes are a result of the erosion of sand and chalk over the centuries. The Surrey Hills is also a place where many historic houses and extensive parklands are open to visitors. Polesden Lacey, once home to Mrs Greville, Clandon Park, the Oslow family seat, Hatchlands Park built for Admiral Boscawen, Loseley Park, seat of the More-Molyneux family, to name a few. They offer highly interesting interiors, immaculately cared for gardens, parklands and spectacular views. Well maintained footpaths in most of the Surrey Hills area allow access to open commons and heathlands, like Frensham Common, Hindhead Common, woodlands like Hurtwood and valleys of

Puttenham Road at the bottom of the Hog's Back.

River Mole at the foot of the Box Hill.

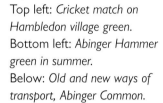

Top left: *Cricket match on Hambledon village green.*
Bottom left: *Abinger Hammer green in summer.*
Below: *Old and new ways of transport, Abinger Common.*

Opposite page:
Top left: *Box Hill shop and café.*
Top right: *National Trust sign at Box Hill on a frosty morning.*
Main: *Hindhead Common and the Devil's Punch Bowl picnic area.*

the Rivers Mole, Tillingbourne and Wey. The National Trusts Dapdune Wharf on the River Wey shows the history of the river's navigation. The Surrey Hills offers spectacular eminences like Leith Hill crowned by the 18th century Gothic Tower, Box Hill with its ancient box trees and chalk downland towering over Mole Gap where the River Mole breaks through the North Downs, Hindhead

The Salomons Memorial at the top of Box Hill

Common and a natural basin of the Devil's Punch Bowl, Newlands's Corner with its famed views over Albury village, Caterham, Gatton, Colley Hill, Pitch Hill, Hascombe, Gibbet and Chinthurst. The agricultural land, covering 40% of the Surrey Hills, consists of many farmsteads creating picturesque patterns of fields divided by well-maintained hedges. The Surrey Hills contains three long distance

Titsey Place mansion.

walks, the North Downs Way, the Greensand Way and the Pilgrims Way. The North Downs Way is a 153 mile long trail starting at Farnham and finishing at the Kent Downs. It follows the chalk scarp in the northern part of the Surrey Hills, which forms the line of the North Downs eastwards close to Guildford, Dorking and Reigate. The legendary Pilgrims Way for much of its length is parallel to the North Downs; pilgrims used it on their way to pay homage at the tomb of Thomas Becket. This way, re-established during Victorian times, leads from Winchester to Canterbury and unlike the North Downs Way, it follows the lanes at the base of the chalk scarp. The Greensand Way running parallel to the North Downs Way alongside the greensand ridge, west of Dorking towards the South Downs, rises at Leith Hill, the highest south-east point at 294 metres. The Greensand Way's 108 mile route goes from Haslemere all the way to Ham Street in Kent. The name of the route comes from the sandstone rock containing green glauconite.

Reigate mill Church.

Gomshall Mill pub, Gomshall.

Rapeseed fields near Wotton.

Opposite: Dapdune Wharf and River Wey in Guildford.

As already observed, the Surrey Hills comprise rich grasslands, ancient woodlands, chalky slopes, acid heaths, extensive vineyards, rivers and ponds. They are all important habitats for wildlife and support varied flora and fauna. Some of the plants that can be found here are bluebells, dwarf milkwort, bedstraw, broomrape, and rare orchids like monkey orchid and man orchid. Among many trees there are oak, beech, whitebeam, hazel, chestnut, pine, hornbeam and birch. Butterflies and insects found here include common blue, green hairstreak, gatekeeper butterfly, Adonis blue and silver spotted skipper. It is also home to many lizards, birds and mammals such as badgers, foxes, squirrels, fallow deer, muntjak and red deer. Woods are represented by ancient woodlands, shaws, old coppice, wooded ghylls, parkland trees, small carrs and conifer plantations. The semi natural habitat is maintained by sheep, ponies, cattle and rabbit grazing. The Surrey Hills boundaries are marked by wooden sculptures carved by artist Walter Bailey. There are two types of sculptures, small wooden signs with the Surrey Hills logo and twelve tall, totem-pole-like sculptures with varied designs. They are positioned in strategic visible places helping visitors to identify the borders of the Surrey Hills AONB and giving the area an identity. The area has some archaeological remains of

Top left: *Clandon Park*.
Bottom left: *Farnham,
The Borough Street*.
Below: *Surrey Hills wooden
sculpture on the A246 road*.

*Opposite: St Catherine's Hill
in Guildford.*

Right: *Loseley Park Manor House.*
Below: *Loseley Park gardens.*

*Old St Peter and St Paul's
church in Albury.*

Neolithic and Mesolithic cultures, defensive forts like Anstiebury, Roman remains like the villa in Farley Green, castles, ruins of Waverley Abbey, many Norman and Saxon churches as well as fortified strongholds. Most characteristic of the area are peaceful villages like Albury, Mickleham, Sheer, Buckland, Brockham, Capel, Wotton and many more. Most of them have Saxon or medieval origins with picturesque pubs, impressive churches and extensive village greens, survivals of the common land with rights to graze animals. London's close proximity has shaped the Surrey Hills area significantly in the 19th and 20th century; with the new railway links, the commuters arrived and settled here, but luckily in most parts the area is still unspoiled.

The stunning scenery of the Surrey Hills AONB boasts a traditional landscape of rolling hills, wooded hillsides and waterways that combine with vibrant market towns, picturesque villages and historic country houses to make it an ideal place to live, work and visit.

Guildford Castle.

Buckland village green.

Chapter 1

Around Farnham

Farnham

FARNHAM IS THE most westerly town in Surrey, sitting on the Hampshire border, in the valley of the River Wey. Narrow picturesque streets and many old buildings make it a very interesting and beautiful town. It is overlooked by Farnham Castle, formerly the home of the Bishop of Winchester. Farnham history is claimed to extend back tens of thousands of years and there is evidence of Stone Age activity as well as some Mesolithic activity some 6000 B.C. Occupation of Farnham continued during the Bronze and Iron Ages, and some Roman and Saxon dwellings were also found here. During the Roman period Farnham became a pottery centre, as clay was abundant. The Saxons gave Farnham the name, Fearnhamme referring to the fern and water meadow. From the year 803, Farnham belonged to the Bishop of Winchester. In 1138 Henry of Blois started to build the castle, which not only provided fortifications, but also accommodation for Bishops, as Farnham was conveniently situated midway between Winchester and London. The castle has been occupied for nearly 900 years and became an important hostelry to a host of monarchs and churchmen. King John, Henry VIII, Queen Elizabeth I, James I, George III, Queen Victoria and many more have visited the place. Queen Elizabeth I extended her stay here to six months. All these visits accelerated the growth of the town bringing prosperity. During the English Civil War, Farnham Castle was besieged and destroyed by Sir William Waller, who was in charge of the Parliamentary troops at the time. On Charles II's restoration, the castle was rebuilt and redecorated to serve as a palace. Until 1927 it remained a residence for the Bishops of Winchester. The castle overlooks the town and consists of the keep and the Bishop's Palace. Farnham Castle management, on behalf of English Heritage, looks after the keep while the Bishop's Palace is under the management of Farnham Castle International Briefing and Conference Centre. Evolving architectural styles left their mark on the castle and today we can see Norman, Tudor and Restoration influences. For centuries, the castle served as a fortress and administration centre while the Palace was the Bishop's accommodation. Henry II built the tower where the original Henri de Blois castle was. The castle is a bailey stone fortress with a motte that was formed around Norman tower foundations. The old tower was enclosed by a circular shell keep with buttress turrets and a gatehouse. In the centre of the castle was a well, which was an important source of water for its occupants. There was also an inner and outer bailey and the inner one contained domestic buildings whilst the outer one was flanked by five towers. One of them was an entrance tower with a drawbridge. At present, only the gatehouse remains. In the Bishop's

Ponies at Hindhead Common and Devil's Punch Bowl.

Farnham, The Borough Street.

Farnham Castle.

Palace, the oldest part is the chapel. Some interesting architectural details are Norman arches and a barrel-vaulted roof. The Great Hall is Norman in origin, dating to around 1180 and had two rows of oak pillars dividing the hall into three isles. In the 17th century Bishop Morley removed the pillars, shortened the hall, raised the walls and added upper galleries. Equally old is the kitchen; of Norman origin it has five characteristic lancet windows and an old fireplace. The Bishop's private room, called Camera, originates from the 13th century. Unfortunately, the stunning scissor beam roof of 1381 is not visible, as it is hidden behind some later alterations. Outside, the gatehouse which is flanked by towers leads into the courtyard. The Waynflete's Tower was built in 1470 and was later modified by Richard Fox in the 16th century and Bishop Morley in the 17th century. The Tudor wing, built for Queen Elizabeth I when she stayed here with her court, has two open galleries running the full length of the house. The Great Stairs between the Great Hall and Bishop's Camera were added by Bishop Morley. The Bishop's Chapel was designed by John Webb in the 17th century. Protestant beliefs of the time are reflected in the stained glass window and wood carving on the walls. The entrance door carvings are supposedly a gift from Louis XIV of France, the "Sun King", to Morley. Both the Palace and the keep underwent extensive restoration and are beautifully preserved. They are Grade I and II listed buildings. A castle wouldn't be a castle without ghosts and as such there is a ghostly monk, a shadowy figure haunting the guard room, a girl dancing on the staircase and an old soldier walking in the cellar! Currently the castle is owned by English Heritage and Farnham Park occupies much of the former castle grounds.

Farnham's wealth came through pottery production and the cloth trade, later followed by becoming one of the greatest corn markets. With the arrival of the railway in 1848, Farnham became a commuter town and a residential district quickly developed. The presence of the Army in the military base at nearby Aldershot benefited the town and significantly increased the number of pubs! Unfortunately many of the original timber-framed buildings were replaced with red brick Georgian town houses; however, many of the Georgian buildings only conceal Tudor structures that continued to survive behind the walls. Farnham Museum is housed in Grade I listed Willmer House in West Street. This 18th-century house has an interesting brickwork façade and solid rusticated pillars. Complementing the building is a walled garden at the back of the house. The name Willmer House comes from the Willmer School for Young Ladies that was here in the 19th century. The museum was opened in 1961 and houses an impressive collection of artefacts associated with the town's history. The museum houses five themed rooms, temporary exhibitions as well as a local studies library. Many school programmes, children's activities and temporary exhibitions take place here. Permanent displays giving insight into the history of town are: "Discover the history of Farnham" and "On the road to Winchester".

Many well-known characters lived in Farnham, including poet and satirist Jonathan Swift, journalist William Cobbett, pamphleteer William Cobbett, John Henry Knight, builder of Britain's first petrol powered car, artist Harold Falkner and J.M. Barrie who wrote *Peter Pan*.

Below left: *Farnham Castle.*
Below right: *Farnham Castle gardens.*

Waverley Abbey

Waverley Abbey was Britain's' first Cistercian Abbey. It was built in 1128 in a peaceful bend of the River Wey, approximately 3 miles south of Farnham. Founded by William Giffard, Bishop of Winchester, it was colonised with twelve monks and an abbot from Aumone in France. The site was unfortunately subject to flooding and the building was damaged as a result. In 1203 new foundations on higher ground were laid and the abbey was rebuilt. The new church was dedicated in honour of

Waverley Abbey.

the Virgin Mary. In 1231 some other buildings, amongst them, a hospital, were added to the site. The total precinct covered an area of about 24 hectares and the surviving ruins date from this period. Waverley Abbey monks and lay brothers were occupied with working the land, organising the wool trade and providing care for pilgrims and the sick. They also produced *Annals of Waverley*, important chronicles from 1066 to 1291. The Abbey grew quickly and became home to two thousand monks in the late 13th century. In later centuries its importance diminished and after the dissolution by Henry VIII in 1536, Waverley Abbey was passed to Sir William Fitzherbert, the King's treasurer. Slowly, all of the buildings were stripped of their decorations, followed by dismantling of the building. Materials from the Abbey were used for building some of the local houses, one of them, the impressive Loseley Park. With very little of the church visible now, it is hard to believe that it used to be an impressive building of 90 metres long and 45 metres wide. Today only parts of the Abbey buildings are standing, mainly the lay brothers' quarters, monks' dormitory, the chapter house, infirmary chapel, the nave, presbytery and the north and south transepts of the church. The most impressive part of the ruins is the lay brothers' refectory with 13th century vaulting supported by very slender columns with simple circular capitals. Also visible is a single traceried window and two pairs of elegant lancet windows. To the east and north of the church some earthworks relating to water management were discovered. The ruined Abbey is managed at present by English Heritage and the site is open to the public free of charge. The remains still give the impression of solitude making it a perfect picnic spot. The Abbey and its perfect positioning by a riverside meadow was an inspiration for Sir Walter Scott's novel *Waverley*; it was also portrayed in Arthur Conan Doyle's romance *Sir Nigel* and featured in many films and television programmes such as *Elizabeth: The Golden Age, Miss Marple, Midsomer Murders*. There are plenty of ghosts and treasure stories connected with the Abbey. Some claim there is a treasure buried in the Abbey grounds, others swear that ghosts of the monks visit the place frequently. The Abbey is situated away from the main road and villages and it is easy to understand how these majestic ruins conjure up monks in white robes praying and chanting in the cloisters – in fact the murmur of the River Wey sounds almost like Gregorian chants! In contrast to the peace and tranquillity of the place, there is some evidence of less peaceful activities of World War II. The entrance to the lush meadow where the monastery stood is guarded by a concrete foundation of a gun emplacement. This site formed part of the defences of London set up in the War. There are also some tank traps by the river, directly behind the Abbey. Despite all that and thanks to the vegetation covering the ruins, the Abbey grounds are indeed peaceful and the Abbey itself is the finest ecclesiastical site in Surrey retains its sense of timelessness.

Facing the ruins is Waverley Abbey House. This beautifully proportioned Georgian house was built in 1723 by Colen Campbell for John Aislabie, the Chancellor of the Exchequer. Later on it was purchased by Florence Nightingale's family. Florence Nightingale, a well-known social reformer and founder of modern nursing was a frequent visitor here. The house stands in the monks' old garden by the 18th century man-made lake with a picturesque bridge. During World War II, a military hospital for five thousand officers was based here; later on the house was used as a nursing home. Today, sympa-thetically restored, it is a training and conference centre of a Christian charitable organisation.

Waverley Abbey bridge.

Waverley Abbey house.

Elstead Mill.

Oxenford Farm near Elstead.

Elstead

Elstead has been occupied by man since prehistoric days as indicated by some earthworks at Charles Hill. The earliest reference to the village is from 1128. Its name, meaning "elder tree place" changed over time from Helstede, Elstede to Elstead. Today it is a lively village with many houses on the north and south side of the River Wey. The ancient monument bridge was built in the 14th century and has five stone arches. St James's church was built in 1138 and was served by priests from nearby Waverley Abbey. It contains 13th-century windows, 14th-century woodwork and a 15th-century oak doorway. The church underwent extensive restoration in 1845. The mill at Elstead, now a popular pub and restaurant dates back to 1649, however there was a corn mill here much earlier, since the 13th century. The original mill was burnt down by Oliver Cromwell's Roundheads who were stationed here. Elstead is surrounded by common land which is used for military training. The area is favoured by film directors, and at Hankley Common as well as at Oxenford Grange Farm, *Robin Hood* directed by Ridley Scott, was filmed.

Tilford Bridge, Tilford.

Tilford

Tilford is a small village in a conservation area two miles south of Farnham. In the heart of the village there is a triangular green with three distinctive oaks; the oldest one called the King's Oak is over 800 years old; the oak commemorating 60 years of Queen Victoria's reign was planted in 1897; and the third one marking the coronation of King Edward VII was planted in 1902. The oak commemorating the accession of King George V in 1910 was unfortunately later uprooted. The main focus on the green is the beautiful Tilford Institute built by Sir Edwin Lutyens in 1894. Through the village the two branches of the River Wey flow and two medieval bridges spanning the river are listed as ancient monuments. Tilford is also home to the Rural Life Centre. The Rural Life Centre is set in over ten acres of garden and woodland. It shows village life as it was in the years 1750 to 1960. The centre was assembled by Mr and Mrs Henry Jackson and is run by a charitable trust. The museum displays a vast collection of tools, devices and machinery used in farming and rural life. There are wheelwrights' tools, village crafts, domestic work and trades including vets, balers and wheelwrights. Purpose built and reconstructed buildings include a post office, a village inn, a chapel, a village hall, cricket pavilion, school room and laundry. The museum highlights farming and all aspects of agriculture, as well as social life of the village from the 19th century. Additional attractions include an arboretum with over 100 species of trees from around the world as well as a narrow gauge light railway operating on Sundays.

Blooming heather on Frensham Common.

Frensham Common

Frensham Common is an area of 400 hectares near Frensham, between Camberley to the north and Hindhead to the south. It is a large expanse of heathland designated as a Site of Special Scientific Interest and Special Protection Area. Some evidence suggests that the area was inhabited for over eight thousand years. There are some Mesolithic and Neolithic finds there as well as Roman and Saxon traces. The area has dry heath, wet heath, open water, reed beds as well as coniferous and mixed woodland. The Common is owned by the National Trust but managed by Waverley Borough

Council. This attractive countryside used to be a source of fuel and building materials and it provided grazing for animals. There are two ponds situated here. The Great Pond and Little Pond were created in the Middle Ages by damming the Whitmore stream, so it could be used for supplying fish for the Bishop of Winchester when he stayed at nearby Farnham Castle. Both ponds support a wealth of wildlife. The Great Pond is used for angling and sailing. It was here in 1913 on the Great Pond, that the very first sea plane was tested. During the Second World War the ponds were drained as they were used as a navigational point by the Luftwaffe. In 1953 Frensham Pond Sailing Club was created. On the Common there is a scheduled ancient monument called the King's Ridge Barrow, a prehistoric bowl barrow, as well as Devil's Jump, a rather unusually shaped hill. The Common supports an important population of insects, reptiles, bats and birds such as nightjars, stonechats, whitethroats, yellow hammers, linnets, siskins, woodlarks and woodpeckers. Frensham Common is not only an important habitat for common and rare wildlife; it is also a valued recreational area. Sandy beaches and the warm water of the ponds are favourite summer spots for families, while open spaces are used for cycling, horse riding, walking and bird-watching. The area is featured in many films, perhaps the most surprising one, being *The Mummy*, where it posed as the River Nile.

Top: *Woods by Little Pond, Frensham Common.*

Above: *Little Pond, Frensham Common.*

Great Frensham Pond.

33

The Sailor's Stone, Hindhead Common.

Hindhead Common in winter.

Hindhead Common

Hindhead Common and the Devil's Punch Bowl are a swathe of woodland valleys and lowland heaths marking the southern gateway to the Surrey Hills. Both areas together cover some 650 hectares of central Surrey and are a significant habitat for heathland-loving animals and birds such as: woodpeckers, warblers, dunnocks, woodlarks, nightjars and stonechats. The Common supports a rich flora, heather, cross-leaved heath, dwarf gorse, common gorse and purple moor grass. Heathland used to dominate the Surrey Hills, but grazing by commoners' animals ended in the mid-1900s. To reverse the consequent spread of birch and bracken, the National Trust reintroduced cattle and Exmoor Ponies to the area. The Devil's Punch Bowl is the best known valley in Surrey. It was given to the National Trust by the Robertson family. The area is steeped in history and there are many legends explaining how this bowl-shaped valley was created. One of them states that the

Devil wanted to annoy the god Thor so he hurled lumps of earth at him. The nearby village Thursley means Thor's Place. There is another story that two giants were scooping the earth and throwing it at each other, one of them missed the throw and created the Isle of Wight, while the hollow became the Punch Bowl. In spite of Lucifer's name being invoked in the name of the place, the truth as to how the valley was created is much less colourful. The valley is the result of water eroding the clay. The area here has a sandstone upper layer and clay beneath. The springs cutting down into the clay made the top sandstone layer collapse. At the very bottom of the valley the stream continues the process even today. Overlooking the valley is Gibbet Hill, the second highest point in Surrey. At 272 metres above sea level it offers stunning views of the Devil's Punch Bowl, Thursley, Hankley Common and even further. On a clear day, the Gherkin, Canary Wharf, the London Eye and Wembley Stadium can be seen. On the summit of Gibbet Hill stands a Celtic Cross. It was erected here by Sir William Erle in 1851 to allay the fears of the local population that evil spirits resided here. Indeed, in the past it was a desolate and dangerous spot favoured by highwaymen. It was also gruesome, as it was chosen as a place of punishment. The criminals were hanged and their bodies covered in tar were left hanging in cages on the gibbets. The crime that shook local people in 1786 was the murder of an unknown sailor. He was travelling to his ship when he met three men whom he treated to a drink. They murdered him and stole his clothing. The murderers were apprehended and executed and their bodies, like all the other criminals, hung on the Gibbet Hill. On the way from the car park to Gibbet Hill stands a stone commemorating this horrible crime while the body of the sailor is buried in Thursley's church of St Michael and All Angels.

With the opening of the London to Portsmouth line, many people settled down in Hindhead and its Hinterland, as they were drawn by easy access to London and the picturesque valley. Among

Above left: *Celtic Cross at Gibbets Hill, Hindhead Common and the Devil's Punch Bowl.*

Above right: *Pony at Hindhead Common and the Devil's Punch Bowl.*

The Devil's Punch Bowl in winter.

them were many writers and poets who found inspiration here: Alfred, Lord Tennyson, George MacDonald, Lewis Carroll, and Arthur Conan Doyle. Many imposing houses were built here, some of them in the Arts & Crafts style. Arthur Conan Doyle lived in Undershaw House in Hindhead, George Bernard Shaw lived at Blen Cathra, scientist John Tyndall in Tyndalls. Some houses are positioned as high as 246 metres above sea level, it is the highest village in Surrey.

The remarkable landscape of Hindhead Common and the Devil's Punch Bowl was divided for many years by a very busy A3, the road running from London to Portsmouth. To relieve traffic congestion in the area and to preserve the sanctuary of the Common's woodland and heathland for the wildlife, 1.8 kilometre twin-bore Hindhead tunnel was designed. It was opened in 2011 at the cost of £371 million. Building it took four and a half years and campaigning over thirty years. The old section of the A3 has been closed and has been returned to nature by the National Trust. The hillside has been re-shaped, the old road buried and heather and grass seeds are spread over the soil. At long last the two areas are reunited with great advantage to wildlife and people.

Thursley

Thursley is a small village on the A3 between Milford and Hindhead. It dates back to Anglo Saxon times. The village name is of Scandinavian origin, meaning "the sacred grove of Thor", Thor being the Norse god of thunder. The local church, St Michael and All Angels dates back to 1100. It has a finely carved 11th-century font and windows containing original oak frames from the same century. In the churchyard there is the gravestone of the unknown sailor murdered in 1786 by three men, Edward Lonegon, Michael Casey and James Marshall as noted above. Thursley is also known for its common which is a National Nature Reserve and Site of Special Scientific Interest consisting of lowland peat bog with rich habitats for insects and birds.

Haslemere

Haslemere, an attractive historic market town, nestles in wooded hills in the south west corner of the Surrey Hills. It is close to the border of Hampshire and West Sussex and is the most southerly town in Surrey. The town marks the western end of the Greensand Way. Haslemere has very old foundations; there are traces of prehistoric settlers as well as Celtic and Romano-British ones. The name of the town comes from the hazel trees surrounding a former lake, which in the past was in the vicinity of the High Street. Although no trace is left of the lake, a spring in West Street was most possibly its source. A rich selection of shops as well as many timbered and tile-hung houses add charm and vibrancy to the east part of the town concentrated around the High Street and to the west part of the town around Wey Hill. Some of the old buildings include Half Moon House, Tudor Cottage next to the Georgian House Hotel and three gabled buildings occupied by Lloyds Pharmacy. In the past the town was quite isolated and only in 1859, when the London-Portsmouth railway was opened, was there a large influx of newcomers whereupon Hindhead quickly became a fashionable place to live. In the High Street a penfold box was introduced by the Post Office in 1866. It was designed by John Wornham. St Bartholomew's church dates back to the 16th century although some historical records show that there was a chapel as early as 1180 A.D. The church was enlarged a few times in 1640, 1816 and in 1871 when it was rebuilt in the Gothic style. Many memorials to prominent residents can be found here.

The Haslemere Educational Museum at the north end of the High Street was founded by eminent surgeon Sir Jonathan Hutchinson in 1888. It was started as a small educational museum in Hutchinson's own home, and it is now housed in a beautiful Georgian House; it is noted for its geological, archaeological and natural history collections and some artefacts from ancient civilisations.

Top: *St Michael and All Angels church, Thursley.*

Above: *Unknown Sailor Stone, St Michael and All Angels church, Thursley.*

There are temporary exhibition rooms, a library and educational rooms. Many interesting workshops, art displays and lectures are organised here.

Haslemere is also known for the annual international music festivals, which are given by the Dolmetsch family who operated in Haslemere a workshop producing early English musical instruments. Haslemere is within easy reach of the Greensand Way, a path leading to the Devils' Punch Bowl and to Kent.

Eashing Bridge

Eashing village situated a couple of miles outside Godalming is first and foremost known for its medieval double bridge. It was built in the 13th century by the monks of Waverley Abbey. This substantial bridge – or rather bridges as they span both the River Wey and its tributary – were built of rubble stone with thin slabs set in mortar. Later on in the 18th and 20th centuries, a brick top and wooden posts were added. A very rare feature of the bridge is that the downstream face of the western portion has rounded cutwaters while the upstream face of the eastern end has pointed cutwaters. Upstream there is a mill and to the left, lovely timbered cottages adding charm to this picturesque place. In 1901, Eashing Bridge was donated to the National Trust and is in its care as a Scheduled Ancient Monument. The bridge recently underwent extensive restoration and it looks as charming as it was portrayed on a very early photograph of Benjamin Brecknell Turner "Eashing

Eashing Bridge

Bridge" taken in 1852 which can be admired in Victoria & Albert Museum. Arguably, it is one of the most charming bridges between Farnham and Guildford, despite it being claimed that at dawn the ghost of the Waverley Abbey monk can be seen wandering about...

Peper Harow

Peper Harow is a tiny tranquil village lying west of the A3. The village is rather unusual as it is privately owned and access to it is restricted. Over the years its name has changed a few times: Pipere-herge, Piperhearge, Piperinges, Pyperhaghe, Pepper Harrow, Peprharo and eventually, Peper Harow, all meaning in Old English a saint's place or pagan temple. The village and the church of St Nicholas have a rich and diverse history. The church dates back to 1301 and in its graveyard there is an ancient yew tree that is possibly over one thousand years old. Many famous people are buried here, amongst them the Viscounts Midleton and General Henry Dalrymple White. The church underwent a massive but sympathetic restoration in the 19th century that was conducted by Augustus Pugin. Peper Harow estate had many owners, some of them in high positions in the royal service. Since 1712 it remained in the hands of the Brodrick family who took the title of Midleton. Peper Harow House was designed by Sir William Chambers and built in 1727. Some other buildings were also designed for the estate are Farnham Lodge, Eashing Lodge, Well House, stables, gate house and other farmhouses. During the Second World War the house was requisitioned for the Canadian Army and some of the old gun emplacements are still visible on the river banks. In the 1970s it served as a residential home for disturbed adolescents and eventually in 1988 the house was converted into flats and became an estate that is not open to the public. Outside the village is a very large granary dated from 1600 resting on 25 wooden pillars. This is a perfect example of old farm building architecture.

Hog's Back

The Hog's Back previously known as Guildown, is the name of the ridge between Farnham and Guildford. The stretch of the A31 alongside the Hog's Back offers spectacular views both south and north. The Hog's Back is raised 154 metres above sea level. The Hog's Back is an ancient ridgeway and it was well documented that it was used to connect Wiltshire with Kent and London to Winchester. To the south the views extend all the way to the Devil's Punch Bowl. On the north side of the Hog's Back, in the old Admiralty Semaphore Station in Poyle Hill Lodge, there is the Ramada Farnham Hotel overlooking the Surrey Downs. In Tongham, just below the Hog's Back, an independent Hog's Back Brewery is situated in the 18th century farm buildings.

The Tern Pond, Puttenham Common.

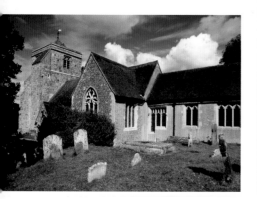

St John's church, Puttenham.

Puttenham

Just south of the Hog's Back, there is a village of Puttenham mentioned in the *Domesday Book* of 1086 as a place belonging to the Bishop of Bayeux. The village is positioned among farmland, woodland and Puttenham Common and it stretches alongside the main road called "The Street". The Common, managed by Surrey Wildlife Trust, is mainly heathland with vividly blooming heather and gorse. Some archaeological finds have been recorded in this area. The church of St John is situated to the east side of the village and is of Saxon origin. The Lady Chapel was added in the 13th century and the tower, in the 15th century. There are some fine 15th and 16th century cottages in the village and next to the church, the Puttenham Priory mansion. This elegant Georgian house dates in origin to 1266. Its Palladian front was added in 1762 by Thomas Parker after the building was extended in 1730. Colour-washed stucco, hipped slate roof, symmetrical Palladian front with five bays, Doric and Ionic columns make a truly impressive mansion and extensive English parkland adds to its beauty. Close to the village is the 16th century sand quarry, which is now disused.

Seale

The picturesque village of Seale is located in a valley, south of the Hog's Back carrying the A31 road between Farnham and Guildford. It also lies on the Pilgrim's Way. The name of the village most probably derives from the Anglo-Saxon for willow. The village is very small and is surrounded by rural environments. Although getting to London or Farnham from here by car is easy and quick, the village doesn't have a station. It doesn't have any shops or pubs either! Some older cottages are situated opposite St Laurence church. Stable Cottage and Manor House Farm are rare examples of buildings of chalk. Although there is plenty of chalk in Surrey and nearby, the Hog's Back is the chalk spine, chalk quarried here is too soft to last long as building material. The Hampton Lodge Estate has been important in the history of the village. Most of the agricultural land here belonged to the Hampton family. The estate was sold in 1929 to Eustace Thornton and is run today by his granddaughter, Bridget Biddell. The beautiful church of St Laurence is partly Norman. The main door as well as the vestry door is Norman. In the 12th century the church was an outpost of Waverley Abbey. The church houses an interesting 12th-century font, a peal of six bells (the oldest one from the 16th century) and a Venetian painting by Cima de Conegliano. The church was restored by J. Croft in 1861-73 in keeping with its medieval style.

Elstead Road near Seale.

St Lawrence Church, Seale.

Guildford Castle.

Chapter 2

Around Guildford

Guildford

GUILDFORD IS LOCATED in the North Downs, where the River Wey breaks through the hills. The exact origins of Guildford are not known but most probably it began as a small Saxon settlement by a ford, after the Romans had removed from Britain. It was referred to as the "Golden Ford" due to the golden sands on the banks of the river, just south of the town. The village turned into a town in the 10th century and by the year 978 was a location of the Royal Mint, which was very important for the town's development. The oldest building in town is St Mary's church. Its tower dates from 1036. Built on the slope, the inside of the church is on three different levels. The church is a mixture of Saxon, Norman and some later styles. In Guildford there are traces of six medieval undercrofts. One of them, at 50-52 High Street built about 1180 is one of the finest examples in the country. Another one is beneath the Angel Hotel on the High Street. These sorts of undercrofts were used as shops possibly selling wine or silk and only rich merchants could afford

River Wey, Guildford.

them, which shows how affluent the town was in medieval times. In the 12th century, a castle was built to the south of the High Street. It is believed that the stone castle built by King Stephen replaced the wooden structure that was built here soon after 1066. Overlooking the ancient ford across the River Wey, it had strategic importance, enabling military control of the east-west route. The castle was built of Bargate stone quarried in nearby Godalming. The motte first acquired a shell keep and later on, a tower. At first, the keep was used as monarch's apartments, later on as sheriff's headquarters and a county jail. Henry III made many improvements to the castle but by the end of the 13th century the castle fell into disrepair. By 1379, only the keep and the great chamber survived. Around and underneath the castle there are some quarries from where the chalk was excavated for many buildings of the town. The passages that are left are called the caverns. By 1611 the ruined castle was sold to a local merchant, Francis Carter and later passed on to Lord Grantley. Eventually in 1855, Guildford Borough Council acquired what was left of the castle. The tower was restored and opened to the public. Inside the tower, the model of the original 13th century castle is displayed and the land around the castle has been transformed into pleasant gardens.

Guildford's main industry in medieval times was trade in wool and clothes. Later on it became a convenient stopping point between London and Portsmouth. In 1619 George Abbot founded what is known as Abbot's Hospital. Born in 1562 in Guildford and educated at the Royal Grammar School that was established here in 1507, he rose to the position of Archbishop of Canterbury. The Abbot's Jacobean alms house on the High Street was a shelter for the old and destitute. Modelled on the Whitgift Foundation it was designed along the lines of an Oxford College and built from first class materials. This fine, three-storey brick building still stands in the same perfect condition 400 years later and offers accommodation to local people. The final resting place of George Abbot is opposite in the Holy Trinity church.

Abbott's Hospital, Guildford.

One of the Guildford landmarks is the Guildhall built in the 1300s and extended through later centuries. Its most prominent feature is the impressive gilded clock of 1683 protruding out over the street. The clock was made by London clockmaker, John Aylward. Guildhall is home to a choice selection of historic paintings and a collection of plates. For centuries Guildford was overshadowed by London but in the 18th and 19th century the town grew rapidly. The Corn Exchange was established here, an iron foundry business built, and both printing and engineering businesses developed. Thanks to the newly established Wey Navigation, goods like flour, timber, coal and gunpowder were transported on the canals, which increased the trade and furthered economic development. In the centre of Guildford, the Dapdune Wharf where canal barges were built was established. Today, the wharf, restored and managed by the National Trust, displays barges and exhibits connected with the Wey Navigation history. In 1845 Guildford was connected by rail to London and this was the base of Guildford's further development in the Victorian Era.

Dapdune Wharf, Guildford.

Guildford is a home to the museum called The Spike. The Poor Law Act of 1834 obliged local magistrates to help the poor by building local workhouses, where the homeless and poor could stay overnight, eat and bathe. In Guildford workhouse inmates were locked for the night in their cells. They were given food but in return, they had to chop wood, pick oakum and break rocks. Today, this Grade II listed building shows the life of the poor and vagrants of the 19th and 20th centuries. Guildford is dominated by its 20th century cathedral, which was designed by Sir Edward Maufe and consecrated in 1961. It stands on top of Stag Hill that was donated by the Earl of Onslow and overlooks the centre of Guildford. This is the only cathedral in Southern England built since the 16th century.

Guildford Cathedral, Guildford.

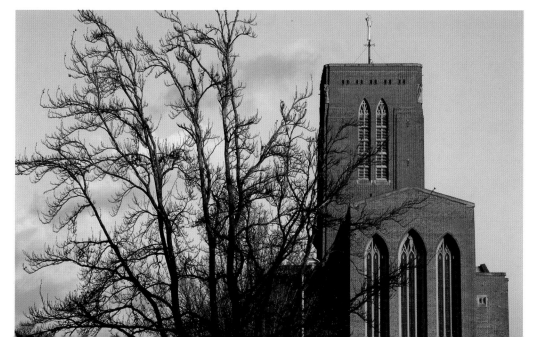

45

Above: *St Catherine's Hill, Guildford.*

Inset: *St Catherine's chapel, St Catherine's Hill, Guildford.*

Downstream on the River Wey on St Catherine's Hill lies St Catherine's chapel. It was built in 1329 by Richard de Wauncey as a chapel of ease for the parishioners living far from St Nicolas church in Guildford. The chapel became disused by 1546 and only outer walls now remain. It is a scheduled monument and ruins are railed off. Sitting high above the river it offers stunning views and is seen from afar. Below it there is Artington Spring that is renowned for its medicinal properties, notably curing sore eyes.

The River Wey flowing through Guildford and many other towns and villages of the Surrey Hills is unusual as it has two separate sources in two different counties, the northern one in Hampshire and the southern one in Surrey. Two branches of the river join at Tilford. The Wey was the very first British river successfully canalised for commercial traffic. It has been used as a source of power for mills that were grinding grain, fulling wool and rolling oats. The river was also used in gunpowder, leather and paper production. In 1653 the River Wey was made navigable for barge traffic and in 1764 it was extended by adding the Godalming Navigation. Commercial traffic included food, gunpowder and many more materials. The idea of the navigation was commenced by Sir Richard Weston, an avid agriculturalist who had witnessed the controlled flooding of pastures in the Netherlands. He put considerable effort into getting the Bill for the construction of the canal presented to Parliament in 1650. In 1651 an Act was passed and extensive works started. The waterways were opened in 1653. Trade continued on the river until 1969 and brought prosperity to the whole region. As the Wey and Godalming navigation required considerable maintenance, the last owners, the Stevens family gifted it to the nation. Since 1964 it has been cared for by the National Trust. This tranquil waterway running through the heart of Surrey offers twenty miles of towpaths for walkers and bikers. These paths were necessary in the past as barges were horse drawn or manually hauled. The river is used for other leisure activities like canoeing and rowing and is an important habitat for wildlife. Alongside it there are many Sites of Special Scientific Interest and Nature Reserves covering a variety of landscapes and environments like water meadows, heathlands and woodlands. On the east bank of the river there is Dapdune Wharf. It was the site of barge building for the Wey Navigations. Today, restored and cared for by the National Trust, it is a museum housing an original barge from 1931 and the *Reliance*, a flat bottomed boat measuring 22 metres long and 4 metres wide. It also hosts many interactive exhibits and displays depicting the story of Surrey waterways.

Far left: *Booker's Tower, Guildford.*

Left: *War Memorial, Guildford.*

Shalford

Shalford village stands near the entrance to the River Wey and Arun Junction Canal, an inland waterway connecting the Thames with the English Channel. Sitting across the clear water of Tillingbourne stream in the village is Shalford Mill, a picturesque watermill. The mill is a perfect reminder of Shalford's industry that was blooming from the Middle Ages to Victorian times. The present mill is an 18th century timber-framed watermill with well-preserved machinery. It ceased operation in 1914. Nothing is known about the early owners of the mill, and the earliest record comes from the 15th century when it was owned by John ate Lee. Later owners from the 16th century onwards were Sir Edmund Walsingham, Sir George More and John Austen. John Mildred who bought the mill in 1751 created the present timber-framed, red-brick-clad building we see today. How the mill survived is quite an interesting story. A group of eccentric, well-educated women, the so called "Ferguson Gang" raised money to buy Shalford Mill, in an attempt to preserve the traditional ways of work and village life. They transferred it to the National Trust in the early 1930s. The mysterious group that saved the mill from demolition used the mill for their clandestine meetings to discuss fund raising for other deserving causes. The Ferguson Gang formed in 1927 was an enigmatic group collecting money to preserve old buildings at risk of demolition. They hid their identities behind masks and used most unusual pseudonyms, including Red Biddy, See Mee Run, Erb the Smasher. Fully masked they used to appear unannounced at the National Trust office depositing monies and instructing how they should be spent. Their notoriety grew, as their mischievous behaviour combined with drama became better known. Wearing masks, chanting Latin verse, using mock cockney, all worked well as PR stunts for their chosen causes; they preserved Shalford Mill, Newton Old Town Hall on Isle of White, Priory Cottage in Oxfordshire as well as many stretches of the beautiful Cornish coastline. Although the mill is no longer functional, its machinery is well preserved and still in its original position. There is a waterwheel, cast iron wheelshaft, wallower spur wheel, three pairs of mill wheels, storage bins and all kinds of ancillary machinery. Visiting the mill provides an interesting insight into an old way of life and its operation.

Bramley

Bramley is positioned 3 miles south of Guildford and was originally a Saxon village. The name means "a clearing in the broom". The oldest building in the village is the church of Holy Trinity that was built around 1100. The tower, chancel and south transept are from the 13th century. The village expanded in the Middle Ages and very significantly later on in the 17th century. It was here on Gosden Common that the very first all-women cricket match was played in 1745 and a plaque marks the occasion. Gertrude Jekyll, the famous garden designer and horticulturalist spent her childhood in Bramley. Millmead House in Snowdenham Lane was designed for her by Edwin Lutyens whilst the garden was designed by her. The village is a conservation area and has many interesting houses.

Wonersh

A settlement in Wonersh has existed since Anglo-Saxon times; the name means "the hamlet in the winding stubble field". Other recorded names in the past were Ognersh and Ignersh. Wonersh used to be a flourishing seat of the weaving and clothing industry which was subsequently followed by agricultural development. There are three listed churches in Wonersh and some notable homes in the village. St John the Baptist is beautifully positioned by the stream, in front of a meadow and it dates back to Norman times. The oldest part of the church is the north wall of the nave. Most probably it was part of the chapel built in 1050. Over the years, the Norman church was enlarged: the tower was added in the 13th century and in the 15th century, the new Guild Chapel. The tall shingled spire was replaced by the present one in 1751. At the end of the 18th century, the church

Chinthurst Hill Tower, Wonersh.

St John the Baptist church, Wonersh.

underwent extensive rebuilding due to extensive decay. The grounds adjacent to the church were given to the village and are known as the Church Green Trust.

The only Grade I listed building in the village is the Tudor moated Great Tangley Manor. The house is over one thousand years old and was mentioned in the *Domesday Book* and used to be a royal hunting lodge. In the 13th century it was turned into a Medieval hall house. Further alternations were carried out in 1582 by Richard Cayall and later on in 1880 when Wickham Flower employed Philip Webb to extend the house. The north wing was added later on by Inigo Thomas. The house has been carefully restored by the current owners and is private property. It is surrounded by extensive gardens containing an alpine garden, a pergola walk, a rock garden and a pretty lake. Famous guests who have visited the house in the past include King George V, Queen Mary, King George VI, Edward VIII, John Evelyn, William Morris and Gertrude Jekyll.

The village is situated between two steep hills, Chinthurst Hill and Barnett Hill. Chinthurst Hill is 121 metres high and is home to the folly tower built in 1930. The woods on the hill are famous for their bluebell display in spring. From the top of the hill there are spectacular views across Guildford, St Martha's Hill and the North Downs. Both the hill and tower are managed by Surrey Wildlife Trust. Barnett Hill is 112 metres high and is occupied by a hilltop Queen Anne style mansion built in 1905 for Frank Cook, the grandson of travel agent Thomas Cook. At present, it is a wedding and conference centre.

Great Tangley Manor, Wonersh.

Loseley Park.

Fields around Loseley Park.

Loseley Park

Loseley Park is an Elizabethan house with extensive gardens and a park. It is situated outside Guildford with stunning views towards the North Downs. It is a residence of the More-Molyneux family. The present house was built between 1562 and 1568 and replaced the earlier medieval one, that Queen Elizabeth I declared inadequate for her to visit! To entertain the Queen in style, a new magnificent mansion was built by Sir William More. To build it, stone from the nearby Cistercian Waverley Abbey was used. The house has changed very little over the years and is mostly the same as in the 16th century. The principal room in the house is the Great Hall containing panelling from the demolished Nonsuch Palace and some precious painted canvas from Henry VIII's banqueting tents. There are also many interesting paintings and tapestries here. The drawing room still has a gilded ceiling decorated for yet another monarch, James I. Other impressive features of the house are a fireplace carved out of a single piece of chalk, the 18th century Vauxhall mirror, and an impressive collection of portraits and books. The walled garden designed by Gertrude Jekyll is a place of calm and beauty. It contains five separate "rooms", the rose garden, the fruit and flower garden, the white garden, the herb garden and the organic vegetable garden. There is also a vine walk, yew hedges and the moat walk. The vast parkland has an ancient mulberry tree, a chestnut avenue leading to the lake and a recent addition is the wildflower meadow. The carefully designed and cared for fine garden and parkland, as well as the historic stately manor with a plethora of artwork and furnishings, makes it one of the most interesting places to visit in the area. The estate has been used in various films and some of the more well-known productions that have been filmed here are *Sense and sensibility*, *Emma*, *Miss Marple* and *Midsomer Murders*.

Watts Cemetery Chapel, Compton.

Compton

Compton village is situated between Godalming and Guildford, just off the Hog's Back. The oldest building in the village is St Nicholas' church that predates Norman times. The church was visited by pilgrims on the way to Canterbury. The nave and chancel were added during the Norman period, as well as pillars and arches carved out of local chalk. An interesting balustrade to the upper sanctuary chapel is the oldest surviving decorative timberwork in Britain. In the north wall there is a hermit cell. The second interesting building in the village is Watts Cemetery Chapel designed by Mary Watts, wife of George Frederic Watts, the Victorian symbolist painter. This mortuary chapel was built in 1896-98 and fully funded by Mary Watts. However, all local villagers were involved in decorating the chapel. Red terracotta brickwork outside and amazing Art Nouveau, Celtic, Romanesque and Egyptian decorations, enriched by Mary Watts original style, make it one of the most unique chapels in the Surrey Hills. Nearby, the Watts Gallery, a purpose-built gallery dedicated to George Frederic Watts' work is open to visitors. The first time the gallery was opened was in 1904 and again in 2011 after an award winning restoration.

Godalming

Godalming has existed since Saxon times when it was given its name which means "of the family of Godhelm". This town is delightfully situated on the picturesque River Wey; the river has been important throughout its history. The *Domesday Book* of 1086 records Godalming as a thriving community with three watermills. With time, the number of watermills increased to eight. The granting of the right to hold a weekly market and an annual fair brought further prosperity to the town. An additional source of income for the town in medieval times was the development of woollen cloth production. When that declined in the 17th century as a result of the industry moving to the north of England, knitting and weaving technology and later on, tanning and leather industries were developed. From the 17th until the 20th century, Godalming continued to thrive on paper making and quarrying of Bargate stone. Due to its position half way between Portsmouth and London, it was a well-established stop point for stagecoaches. In 1764 trade received yet another boost, this time with the opening of the Godalming Navigation. Connecting the town with the Wey Navigation at Guildford enabled the shipment of bulk goods and furthered the town's prosperity while the advent of the railway in 1849 transformed the place into a popular commuter town. Godalming was the very first town in the world to have public electricity installed in 1881 and although it reverted to gas a few years later, electricity returned here in 1904. Today, Godalming is a very pretty town with narrow picturesque streets lined with many Tudor timber-framed buildings and some elegant 17th century historic brickwork buildings. There are over 138 listed buildings here, a large number of them

Tudor cottages, Mill Lane, Godalming.

The Pepperpot, Old Town Hall, Godalming.

in the High Street and Church Street. One of the most characteristic buildings is the Town Hall. It was built in 1814 and is popularly known as the Peper Box or Pepperpot. Pepperpot is the symbol of Godalming and replaces a former timber medieval market house that stood here. A one storey building with a small square turret housing the clock was designed by a local architect named Mr Perry. Although the building is not used any more for council meetings, any important public announcements, such as Royal Proclamations still take place here. Godalming Museum occupies the oldest historic building. This medieval place dates to 1446. There are interesting displays of paintings, ceramics, designs and embroidery, especially rich in the Arts and Crafts section. The museum houses works of Sir Edwin Lutyens and Hugh Thackeray, both Arts and Crafts artists, with a strong emphasis on the work of Gertrude Jekyll, the garden designer for Edwin Lutyens who was so prolific in South West Surrey. Both, Edwin Lutyens and Gertrude Jekyll were well versed in local vernacular and embraced the ideals of the Arts and Crafts movement in their planting and designs. The Arts and Crafts movement was not about a particular style but more of a philosophy, advocating the use of local materials and taking inspiration from nature and believing in solid handcraftsmanship. The main church of Godalming is St Peter and St Paul, which dates back to the 9th century. The north and south chapels were added in the 13th century. The church is beautifully positioned by the water meadows, but still close to the centre of town. Many of the original features survived and are well preserved.

Witley Common.

Witley

Witley is a small village situated 5 miles south of Godalming. There are some attractive cottages and some 19th century houses in the conservation area of the village. The church of All Saints is picturesque and has Saxon windows and interesting 12th century painting of the Virgin. The village is close to Witley and Milford Commons which are designated as a Site of Special Scientific Interest. This extensive heathland and woodland used in previous centuries as a common land for grazing animals and turf cutting is a rich habitat for birds and insects. It also features some ancient burial mounds from the Bronze Age. During both World Wars it was used as an army training camp. The Commons are managed by the National Trust and all the footpaths and bridleways are well marked. The most fascinating story connected with Witley is the story of Witley Park, previously under the name of Lea Park. The entrance to Witley Park is marked by Milford Lodge Gatehouse on the road from Milford to Haslemere. Although the manor of Witley has had many royal connections and played an important role in local history, only in the 19th century did it gain notoriety. James Whitaker Wright bought nine thousand acres of land in Haslemere and Hindhead and developed the existing house into a 32 bedroom mansion. His house was packed with treasures from across the world and gardens decorated with many impressive statues. As if that was not enough, there was also a theatre, a velodrome, an observatory, stables for fifty horses and a private hospital. Most famously, he had built three artificial lakes as well as a boathouse designed by Lutyens and a spectacular underwater ballroom that catches the imagination even today. The entrance to the underwater world is through a secret door in the wood, a staircase and a flooded tunnel. At the end of the tunnel there is the domed ceiling of the ballroom. A giant Neptune statue situated on top of the dome emerges from the surface of the lake. All of this was paid for by this self-made millionaire, who promoted himself as an expert in mining ventures. He had persuaded many people into investing in his schemes. Some illegal practices and manipulating of share prices soon caught up with him and his company became insolvent sending shockwaves through the mining industry, bankrupting many people. For his illicit actions and defrauding in the region of £640 million in today's money, he was sentenced to seven years imprisonment. Instead of facing punishment, he chose a spectacular exit and killed himself by cyanide poisoning. He is buried in All Saints church in Witley. His estate was parcelled up and sold off after his death. Lord Pirrie, the designer of *Titanic* became the new owner of the mansion. Unfortunately the mansion has not survived, as in 1952 it burned down. Today the park is in private hands and Hindhead Common was bought by local residents and handed over to the National Trust.

Witley Common.

Hambledon

Hambledon is a small and scattered village tucked amongst fields and woodlands near Godalming. The village appeared in *Domesday Book* of 1086 as Hameledune. There are several interesting buildings scattered in the village, such as the Old Granary, the School Cottage, Court Farm as well as the church. Nothing is left of the 11th century village church but the present day 19th century church of St Peter contains some traces from the 14th century. Next to the village green amongst some picturesque cottages is Oakhurst Cottage, a small 16th-century labourer's dwelling. This simple timber frame cottage has been lovingly restored by the National Trust and can be visited in the summer by appointment only. Inside you will find some simple furnishings and everyday objects on display. Outside, a small garden displays typically Victorian plants. Nearby, at Hydon's Ball Hill, there is a memorial to Octavia Hill, one of the National Trust founders. Hambledon is also home to some delightful llamas. The Merry Harriers offers a unique opportunity to walk with llamas in Surrey Hills. These lovely animals whose origins go back some 40 million years are incredibly intelligent and affectionate and a walk with them followed by a picnic or lunch at the very first llama's pub in the UK is a joy.

"Daisy" Cottage in Hambledon village.

Crown Inn, Chiddingfold.

Chiddingfold

The small but beautiful village of Chiddingfold probably existed before the Norman Conquest. The site of a Roman villa was discovered in a field near the village. Some pottery, ornaments and foundations found here indicate Roman settlement. The village name recorded as Chedlingefelt, meaning the fold (enclosure for animals in the hollow) was first mentioned in 1130. It wasn't recorded in the *Domesday Book*, as it was most probably part of Godalming Manor. Chiddingfold's prosperity came from iron founding, agriculture, wool and cloth making as well as glass making from the 13th to the 16th century. Its international importance as a glass making centre was possible thanks to eleven glass works that were established here. Glass from here was ordered for St Stephen's chapel at Westminster in 1351 and St George's chapel at Windsor. The glass works were closed during the reign of Elizabeth I as the inhabitants of the area complained that furnaces were causing a nuisance. The village is centred on the village green pond. Most buildings here date from the 14th to the 16th century and are mostly timber framed with tile hung elevations, high pitched gables and imposing chimneys. Among these old buildings, the Crown Inn was established in 1285. It is not only one of the most picturesque buildings but is also one of the oldest inns in England. It was established for Cisterian monks on their pilgrimage from Winchester to Canterbury. Some of the distinguished visitors here include Edward VI in 1552 and Queen Elizabeth I in 1591. The village church of St Mary that is situated alongside the Green is a Grade I listed building; it is a 12th century building that replaced an earlier wooden chapel. The church was extended in 1230, 1330, 1450 as well as in the 17th century. A major restoration took place in 1869 and throughout the 20th century. Some of its most interesting features are unique lancet windows made of Chiddingfold stained glass from 1226 to 1612, two piscinas of 1230 and 1260 as well as two 13th century doorways. Situated close to Chiddingfold, the Ramster Gardens offer a mature woodland garden with many rare trees, shrubs and wildflowers. Famous for its spring display of blooming rhododendrons, azaleas, camellias and magnolias, it also attracts visitors to its lakes and ponds.

Dunsfold

Dunsfold is a small village close to the Sussex border; the first settlement here started in the 12th century. The name derives from Saxon times meaning an enclosure on a hill. Earlier names were Duntesfaude, Dutesfaud and Duntesfalde. By the 16th century the village was the site of three ironworks and later on, gunpowder works and glass works. In later years the village benefited from the trade generated from the construction of the Wey and Arun Canals. Dunsfold has houses of architectural interest, many of them from the 17th century when they were built by Londoners escaping the Great Plague. The Common House is the second oldest building in the village and it dates from 1500. The oldest building is the Norman parish church of St Mary and All Saints. It was called "the most beautiful country church in all England" by William Morris. It has an idyllic rural setting half a mile from the village, elevated above a tributary of the River Arun. The church is unique as it is built in one uniform style dated to 1260. The rafters of the roof still retain patterns painted in 1280. The outside walls of the church are made of Bargate stone and the oak door is dated to the 14th century. Inside the church the oak pews are some of the oldest in England and date to the 13th century. In the large churchyard there are some ancient, 1500 year-old yews. The lych-gate is a memorial to Queen Victoria and was erected in 1901. Close to the church is a pre-Christian Holy Well which has a reputation for miraculous cures for eye diseases. Near the village, during World War II, the Canadian Army built an emergency landing airfield. Operating from Dunsfold were Mosquitoes, Spitfires, Typhoons, Mustangs and B-25 Mitchell Bombers. In the years 1948-49 it played a part in the Berlin Airlift. In 1950, the Hawker Aircraft Company leased the place and used it as a flight test centre and development site for Hunter jet fighter, Sea Hawk and Sea Fury planes. Until the 1990s, the aerodrome was screened from public gaze and was protected by the Official Secrets Act. Eventually, British Aerospace sold the place in 2002 to the Royal Bank of Scotland and the Rutland Group. Dunsfold Park, as it is known now is used as an unlicensed airfield and as a test track. It was used for filming *Top Gear*, James Bond *Casino Royale*, *The Da Vinci Code* and many more movies. The owners of Dunsfold Park proposed to build a new eco-town here but the proposal was rejected in 2009.

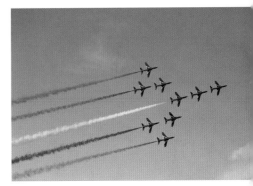

Planes at the annual Dunsfold air show 'Wings and Wheels'.

Winkworth Arboretum.

Winkworth Arboretum

Winkworth Arboretum is a National Trust-owned arboretum situated near Godalming. It was established in the 20th century by Dr Wilfrid Fox, an outstanding dermatologist with a passion for trees and bushes. This enthusiastic gardener bought some land in a relatively neglected corner of Surrey in 1937 and proceeded to create an arboretum. Today it houses over one thousand different shrubs and trees, many of them rare species. He allowed access to the public from the outset and in 1952 gave all 62 acres of land, including the upper lake which has a picturesque wooden boathouse, to the National Trust. Although Dr Fox initially concentrated on maples, later on he planted various Japanese cherries, magnolias, rhododendrons and azaleas which create an impressive display of colour in the spring as well as in autumn. Winkworth is also famous for its carpet of bluebells in the springtime.

Left and above: *Boathouse in Winkworth Arboretum.*

Cranleigh

Cranleigh is located midway between Guildford and Horsham and is reputed to be the largest village in England. Its name derives from the cranes which were bred here as delicacies for the King. The figure of a crane can be found in the Fountain Square, where it adorns the old drinking fountain of 1874. The village escaped the damage of the Civil War, as Oliver Cromwell stayed here at Knowle House. Cromwell Coffee House that is popular with locals and visitors keeps his name alive even today. The oldest building in the village is St Nicholas' church, which dates back to 1170. Later in the 12th century the original church was extended, side aisles and a tower were added, followed by the chancel that was built in the 14th century. The church was extensively restored in 1847. Most buildings in the village are from the 19th and 20th centuries. An important role in the development of the village was played by Stephen Rowland who formed Cranleigh Gas Company in 1876, added mains for water supply in 1886 and a few years later, laid out many streets in the village. Cranleigh has many traditional shops, bakeries and tea rooms, but also some larger supermarkets making this a rural yet modern location. The village possesses a unique hospital; it was opened in the 1850s and still serves the local community. The charming maple trees on the High Street were planted in 1890. In and around the village there are many highly varied footpaths, including the Downs Link footpath, the Greensand Way and the Sussex Border Path. All that makes it a delightful village and a popular place to live and visit.

Chilworth

The village of Chilworth is situated in the valley of the River Tillingbourne, 3 miles southeast of Guildford. The river was a key factor in the village's prosperity, as a paper mill, a wire mill and a gunpowder factory were situated here. The gunpowder estate was established in 1625 by the East India Company and today it is an English Heritage Scheduled Monument with its entrance off Blacksmith Lane. Today it is mostly ruins, but in the 17th century, there were eighteen water powered stamp mills for incorporating gunpowder and some coal and brimstone mills for grinding the ingredients. The Upper Works were closed at the end of the 17th century and the Lower Works became paper mills. In the middle of the 19th century, some steam powered engines were built and at the end of the 19th century, it became a smokeless powder factory. During the First World War cordite works were added, but all were closed in 1920. Chilworth Manor, a Grade II listed building situated just above Chilworth used to be a monastery until Henry VIII's dissolution. From 1580, it was owned by William Morgan and later on by the Rondyll family, followed by Richard Houlditch and the Duke and Duchess of Marlborough. There are other interesting houses in the area, for example, Powder Mill from 1606, Potsford House from 1806, Tangley Mere from 1851, Lockner Holt from 1860 and Brantyshay from 1885.

Chilworth Gunpowder Mills.

Opposite: *View from St Martha's Hill.*

Overlooking the village is St Martha's Hill that reaches a height of 175 metres. The hill commands splendid views all the way to Newlands Corner. Two rights of way, the Downs Link and the North Downs Way intersect here and offer wonderful scenery. At the summit is situated the church of St Martha-on-the-Hill. This remote church on the ancient Pilgrim's Way was rebuilt on the 12th century ruins in 1848 in Norman style. It used to be the site of an Iron Age hill fort and no wonder, as from this spot, eight different counties can be seen on a clear day. To worship or attend concerts, people have to climb the hill, as there is no access to the top by car. It takes a steep fifteen minute walk from Halfpenny Lane, but it is well worth it.

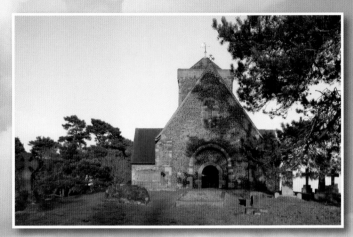

St Martha-on-the-Hill church, St Martha's Hill.

St Martha-on-the-Hill churchyard, St Martha's Hill.

St Martha's Hill view from Chinthurst Hill.

Albury

The pretty village of Albury situated at the south side of the North Downs is best known for the picturesque Saxon church featured in the film *Four Weddings and a Funeral*. The old St Peter and St Paul's church is positioned in the original old village of Albury, within Albury Estate. The new village with its ornate chimneys lies a mile to the west of the old church. The village neighbours two hamlets, Farley Green and Little London. Overlooking the village is Newland's Corner, famous for its spectacular views over the Surrey Hills. Through the village runs the River Tillingbourne. The old

Sunrise at Newlands Corner.

Old St Peter and St Paul's Church in Albury.

New St Peter and St Paul's Church, Albury.

St Peter and St Paul's church is a redundant Anglican church that is under the care of the Churches Conservation Trust. It is a Grade I listed building that once stood in the middle of Albury village. The owners of the large county mansion built on the site of a Tudor Manor House decided to develop a park around it, so the villagers were moved to the hamlet off Weston Street, which in time became the present village of Albury. The old church is no longer used but can still be visited throughout the year. The building dates from Saxon and Norman times. The amazing entrance door dates from the 13th century and on the opposite wall to the door, there is a faint painting of St Christopher dating to the 15th century. The south aisle was added in the 14th century and the north porch in the 16th century. The 17th century spire of the church was damaged unfortunately and replaced with the current cupola. The south transept of the church has been transformed by August Pugin into the highly decorative mortuary chapel for the Drummond family who owned Albury Park Estate from 1819.

The new St Peter and St Paul's church is a red brick imposing building that stands on the hill overlooking the village. It was designed by William Macintosh Brookes and built for Henry Drummond in 1839, an eccentric banker and parliamentarian, as a replacement for the old church.

Silent Pond near Albury.

Fields near Newlands Corner.

At the same time, Drummond was involved with the foundation of yet another church in the village, the Apostolic church, loosely associated with Edward Irving's preaching. The church was also designed by William Macintosh Brookes yet this one however followed the Gothic style. It sits across the Tillingbourne River, in sight of Albury Mansion and is visible from the road leading to Albury village. Albury Mansion lies within the Albury Estate which is owned by the Duke of Northumberland. Gardens around the mansion were designed by the well-known landscape gardener John Evelyn at the turn of the 18th century. The mansion was built on the site of a Tudor Manor House in the 18th century. Later on, the house was significantly redesigned by John Soane and by Augustus Pugin for Henry Drummond. The house underwent many changes over the years. The mansion at present is a Grade II listed building and is divided into private apartments. The house's most striking feature is a collection of 63 candlestick chimneys designed by Pugin based on Tudor originals. Albury village's charm and history are not the only assets that draw tourists and visitors here. The village is in close proximity to lovely Silent Pool and Newlands Corner. Newlands Corner is a popular beauty spot situated on the ridge of Albury Downs commanding some of the best views over the Surrey Hills. This part of the North Downs reaches a height of 170 metres. There are the open chalk downs and mixed woodland to explore and below the slope, across the fields, lies the village of Albury with its characteristic red brick church. Together with the Silent Pool it is owned by Albury Estate and managed by Surrey Wildlife Trust. Silent Pool and neighbouring Sherbourne Pond are spring fed lakes at the foot of the North Downs, set back from Shere Road. The water feeding the lake is crystal clear due to the natural filtration through the chalk. Sheltered by towering trees, this unusually quiet place has been a popular place to visit since Victorian times. A regular visitor to this slightly eerie and charming place was the celebrated poet, Lord Tennyson. Legend has it that a young woman drowned in the pond and her pale figure floats on the surface from time to time. The young maiden who haunts the pond is Emma, a local woodman's daughter who went bathing in the lake. She was spotted by King John who advanced upon her. Forced into the deep water, she lost her footing and drowned. Archbishop Stephen Langton, who was born in nearby Friday Street, upon hearing about the terrible death of Emma wanted to prove that nobody, not even the King is above the law, and he therefore led a group of barons who forced King John to sign the Magna Carta in 1215. As lovely as the story is, it is mainly based on a legend revived by Martin Farquhar Tupper in 1887 in his book *Stephen Langton, a Romance of the Silent Pool*. Interestingly, the Silent Pool was a place where another mystery, the disappearance of Agatha Christie in 1926 took place. Following a marital row, the famous novelist wrote to the Deputy Chief Constable in Surrey claiming that her life was in danger. Her abandoned car was found at the Silent Pool car park. For many hours and days officers and civilians searched for her, without any result. Even Arthur Conan Doyle joined the search contacting a spiritual medium, but for 11 days there was no trace of her. She was discovered staying at the Swan Hydropathic Hotel in Harrogate, safe and sound, posing as a South African lady and claiming amnesia. Whether it was her revenge on an unfaithful husband, Archie Christie or true amnesia, we will never know.

Below left: *Ornate chimneys in Albury.*

Below right: *Catholic Apostolic church in Albury.*

Foundations of a Roman villa at Farley Heath, Farley Green.

Farley Green

The small hamlet of Farley Green is set on high ground to the south of Albury and south east of Guildford. It spreads alongside Shophouse Lane towards Winterfold Forest. The village is very rural and remote in its character. The local church of St Michael is in the charming 19th century barn. This remote area was in the past the haunt of smugglers and in the not so distant past, it was here that the money from the Great Train Robbery was discovered in the local forest. The heathland on the outskirts of the village is the site of the largest Roman settlement in Surrey. The building from the 1st century AD, now marked by stones, was discovered by local antiquarian and poet, Martin Tupper. Many of the artefacts from the dig are in the British Museum, but the foundations are still clearly visible.

Shamley Green

The picturesque village of Shamley Green is situated midway between Guildford and Cranleigh. It lies in the parish of Wonersh and the nearest villages are Blackheath and Farley Green. This semi-rural village has many old listed timber-framed buildings and surrounding farmlands and heaths add to the village's charm. At the centre of the village is the cricket green, the pond and two pubs, the Red Lion and the Bricklayers Arms. Christ Church dating from 1863 is situated on the edge of the village. One of the charming houses in Shamley Green is the 16th century Winter's Grace, where Alfred Hitchcock lived for ten years. He bought the house in 1928 and although he later moved to California, this house must have been important to him as he named his television company "Shamley Productions". The great director's mother lived next to Winter's Grace until her death in 1942.

Blackheath

Blackheath village was established around 1833 and soon grew rapidly as the cottages here were built for the workers of the nearby gunpowder works. The largest property in the village is the Friary of the Franciscan order established here in 1892. St Martin's village church was designed by Charles Harrison Townsend and built in 1892 by local builders Messers Brown of Bramley. It was based upon an Italian wayside chapel. The design is unusual and for some it may look like a barn, but without a doubt, the squat stuccoed and buttressed walls and the round-headed entrance arch as well as pantile roof with bell turret, make this building striking.

On the edge of the village there are woods and the heath. Some parts of Blackheath are designated Sites of Specific Scientific Interest. The heath, cultivated in the Bronze Age is characterised by poor sandy soils and inhabited with heather and gorse bushes. The gradual loss of heath over the years is being reversed by correct management of the common by removal of encroaching woodlands and protecting the invaluable sites used by birds, butterflies, snakes and lizards. It was on this heath that troops staged a military exercise for Queen Victoria in 1864. Unfortunately the spectacle was marred by an accident when the local vicar was shot and killed.

Blackheath Common.

St James's church, Shere.

Forge, Shere village.

Shere

Shere is one of the most beautiful villages in the Surrey Hills. It is quite a small village but full of traditional English features; old tea shops, classic pubs, a blacksmith, an ancient church and a picturesque stream running through the village. Shere's church, St James, is of Norman origin and is approached through the lych-gate that was designed by Edwin Lutyens in 1902. The church was originally built in 1190 and most of it is from the 12th to the 14th century. Connected with a church is an intriguing story of Christine Carpenter who decided in 1329 to devote her life to God; her wish was to be enclosed in a cell built into the chancel. She was receiving the eucharist through a squint and food through a metal grating on the outside wall. Most Shere cottages are from the 16th and the 17th century although there are some as old as the 15th century. The White Horse Inn opposite the Church Square was built in 1450 and the William Bray was built in the 18th century. There are also many other interesting houses: the Old Forge, the Old Prison, the Weavers House, Netley House, the Wheelright Cottage as well as the Old Fire Station that has been converted into public toilets. The Shere Museum is in the Malt House and contains documents and pictures of local history. Through the centre of the village runs the River Tillingbourne. The Tillingbourne rises near Leith Hill and has four principal tributaries: the Friday Street stream, the Holmbury St Mary stream, the Sherbourne Brook and the Law Brook. The river was used in the past in the gunpowder and paper industries as well as to power the flour mills. Today, the river is used for trout farming, watercress beds and for growing reeds. With so much beauty, it is not surprising that the quaint village was a location for many films, such as *The Holiday* and *Bridget Jones: the Edge of Reason* and its tranquillity has attracted many visitors.

Gomshall

Gomshall village, once an important centre for the tanning and leather industry, appeared in the *Domesday Book* of 1086. Neighbouring villages include Shere, Albury and Abinger Hammer. Smaller and more modest than Shere, it is still picturesque with a large selection of Victorian cottages. The River Tillingbourne running through the village enabled the development of many local industries like tanning, watercress growing and, perhaps the most important, milling in the past. Gomshall Mill was mentioned in the *Domesday Book*, but the current mill dates from the 17th century and contains some original milling machinery. The mill changed hands numerous times and continued to work until 1953. After that date it was converted into a shop, and later on a restaurant and a tea room. The village today is famous for its antique and crafts shops.

Gomshall village.

Clandon Park.

Clandon Park

Clandon Park is an early 18th-century Palladian mansion built by Venetian architect Giacomo Leoni for the 2nd Earl of Onslow. It sits in extensive parkland in West Clandon, just outside Guildford. The house replaced an Elizabethan property that once stood here. The Onslow family have lived at Clandon Park since 1641; the family moved from Shrewsbury to London and over the centuries many members of the family have followed political careers. Richard Onslow, known as the Black Speaker, became Speaker of the House of Commons in 1566, Richard Onslow II was elected

Speaker in 1708 and Arthur Onslow was elected Speaker in 1728 and became known as the Great Speaker. Clandon Park was given to the National Trust in 1956 when Lady Iveagh bought it from her nephew, the 6th Earl of Onslow. The mansion's magnificent interiors have many of its original Palladian and Baroque features and fine Italian plasterwork depicting scenes from mythology. The two-storey Marble Hall contains marble chimney pieces by sculptor Michael Rysbrack and is one of the finest such rooms in Europe. The house contains an impressive collection of 18th century furniture, porcelain, textiles, tapestries and carpets. It also houses the Queen's Royal Surrey Regiment Museum. The gardens landscaped by Capability Brown in 1781 contain a grotto, a formal parterre and the sunken Dutch Garden that was created by Frances, Countess of Onslow in the 19th century. The Dutch Garden contains a Memorial for British Airways Air Cabin Crew. In the garden stands Hinemihi, a Maori meeting hut brought here from New Zealand in 1892 by the 4th Earl of Onslow, who was Governor of New Zealand from 1889-1892. The hut provided shelter to Te Wairoa village during the eruption of Mount Tarawera in 1886.

Maori meeting house, Clandon Park.

Hatchlands Park

Hatchlands Park is a beautiful house and estate near East Clandon. The park was originally the property of Chertsey Abbey and after the Dissolution of the Monasteries was granted to Sir Anthony Browne. The red brick country house was built for Admiral Edward Boscawen, hero of the battle of Louisburg, who bought the estate in 1750. The Boscawens employed the architect Stiff Leadbetter to build the house and landscape the grounds. Interior design is the work of the architect Robert Adam; he decorated the house in a nautical style with dolphins, sea nymphs and anchors to reflect the owner's connection with the sea. After the Admiral's death, Hatchlands was sold to the Sumner family. George Sumner and later on his son, commissioned Humphry Repton and Joseph Bononi to improve the house and the grounds. In 1888 the estate was sold to Lord Rendel. His family continued to live here until the 1950s. Rendel made further alterations to the house and garden. Some Rococo decorations as well as the music room were added, while famous gardener, Gertrude Jekyll designed the garden with a parterre laid out in four squares framed with oblong and cornered beds. Lord Rendel's grandson, Harry Stuart Goodhart-Rendel gave Hatchlands to the National Trust in 1945. Today the mansion is open to the public and houses a fine collection of English, Italian, Flemish and Dutch paintings as well as the world's largest collection of composer-related keyboards instruments. There are 18 instruments owned or played by Frédéric Chopin, Johann Christian Bach, Wolfgang Amadeus Mozart and many other composers. The Alec Cobbe Collection, as it is called, has around 50 keyboard instruments dating from 1750 to 1840, one of them, a pianoforte, was reputedly made for Queen Marie Antoinette. The instruments are maintained in pristine condition and there are some concerts held during the open season.

Hatchlands Park.

East Horsley

East Horsley

East Horsley is a village situated between Leatherhead and Guildford. Listed in the *Domesday Book* as "Horslei", it later became known as Lovelace Village in the 19th century. Many changes to the village were introduced by William Currie, who bought property here in 1784. He rebuilt many of the houses and has restored the local church. After his death, a large gothic mansion was bought by the First Earl of Lovelace. His wife, Ada, was Lord Byron's daughter. She was a writer and mathematician, famous for her notes on the Analytical Engine that was recognised as the very first algorithm for machine processing. Lovelace was quite eccentric in his architectural ideas and transformed the houses in the village in a unique style using flint and decorative terracotta bricks and tiles. His home, Horsley Towers, is a Victorian Gothic mix and its main feature is the steeply roofed tower. Guildford Lodge which is visible from the A246 and the other 50 buildings all have very distinctive characters. He also stamped his architectural signature in the nearby woods where he had built 15 bridges, all individually designed and handcrafted. Lovelace is buried in the churchyard of St Martin's church. The church has some interesting 13th century features, and Lovelace mausoleum is in his favourite style with terracotta brickwork. Today, Horsley Park, Lovelace's idiosyncratic home, is a luxurious De Vere hotel with training and conference facilities.

Chapter 3

Around Dorking

Dorking

DORKING TOWN nestles at the heart of the Surrey Hills on the greensand, between the chalk of the North Downs and the clay of the Weald. Originally a staging post on Roman Stane Street, it turned into a market centre for the surrounding villages. By the 15th century it was a prosperous agricultural market town. The famous Dorking fowl were sold here at the corner of South Street and Butter Hill. Introduced by the Romans, this five-toed breed has excellent meat and eggs and was favoured by many, including Queen Victoria. The cockerel symbolising this breed was incorporated into the town's coat of arms and a rather large statue stands by the entrance to Dorking, on Deepdene roundabout. Following the arrival of the train in 1867, many Londoners chose to build their houses here, in the pleasant environment of Dorking, close to unspoiled countryside. The area also became fashionable for recreation due to nearby Box Hill, the North Downs, Mole Valley and Norbury Park. Despite all the expansion over the years, Dorking has managed to retain a quiet and charming character. There are three main streets, the High Street, West Street and South Street, with many interesting structures. There is an eclectic mix of Victorian and Edwardian buildings, but also some medieval ones, including notable hostelries, for example The Bull's Head and White Horse Hotel. Dorking is famous for its plentiful antique shops in its historic West Street, but it also offers a modern open air shopping centre, St Martin's Walk with plenty of shops and restaurants. Dorking Museum behind West Street is located in the Stockhouse; the building was converted during the 1820s into a foundry, where Dorking's gutter grates were made. Maps, newspapers, and books connected with the town are housed here. There is also an extensive fossil collection, early agricultural machinery and house equipment housed in the machine shop on the other side of the courtyard.

Dorking parish church is St Martin's. Its 210 feet spire built as a memorial to Samuel Wilberforce is one of the tallest in the county and is visible for miles. This fine 19th century church was designed by Henry Woodyer and built on an ancient religious site. Dorking is famous for its multilevel caves that are manmade. These 17th and 18th century caves were created by excavations of sand and used as cellars and storage places by smugglers and later on by shop owners. The entrances from South Street

Opposite: *Hurtwood off Radnor road, near Peaslake.*

are sealed but the caves can be visited on Heritage Open Days. The caves are worth visiting for the unique graffiti from the 17th, 18th and 19th centuries. Dorking town with its strong sense of history and tradition celebrates each year the Leith Hill Music Festival. This tradition of a series of concerts has continued for over 100 years, with a strong emphasis on local composer, Ralph Vaughan Williams. Dorking and places nearby were an inspiration for many writers and musicians. It was the birthplace of actor Laurence Olivier, artist Walter Sadler, home to composer Ralph Vaughan Williams, and architect Thomas Cubitt. Charles Dickens set part of *The Pickwick Papers* in Dorking, Jane Austen was a regular visitor here and Daniel Defoe wrote about the local places – no wonder as the area is noted for its beauty and Dorking has its own special appeal and identity.

Denbies Estate

To the north-east of Dorking, overlooking the slopes of Box Hill, Denbies Estate is England's largest single estate vineyard boasting 265 acres of vines. The estate offers amazing views towards Leith Hill and the Tillingbourne Valley. The estate is named after John Denby, an early owner of the farm. In 1754 he sold the farm to Jonathan Tyers, owner of Vauxhall Gardens in London. On this newly purchased area he created a country seat for himself and in 1761 he opened the New Spring Gardens. There were walks, pavilions, illuminations, but in contrast to his famous frivolities of Vauxhall, the gardens were decorated with many reminders of death, including statues of the Christian and the Unbeliever, human skulls and other memento mori objects. It was a popular garden and even Prince Albert paid a visit, however, the tree that was planted by him; unfortunately did not survive the 1990 Great Storm. In 1850 the estate was bought by Thomas Cubitt, the builder of a significant part of London. Here, he has constructed a grand Italianate mansion with almost 100 rooms. When the upkeep of the house became impossible, Cubitt's great grandson demolished the house in 1953 and converted the laundry and gardener's house into a Regency style residence for himself. Denbies Estate was sold in 1984 to a businessman called Adrian White who was persuaded to plant vines, as the soil and climate of the hill is similar to that of Champagne in France. It was also discovered that the Romans planted vine very close to the estate. The venue proved to be very successful and up to 400,000 bottles of fine sparkling wine and table wine in a good year are produced here using traditional methods with modern equipment. Some of the more popular varieties grown here are: Seyal Blanc, Reichensteiner, Ortega, Chardonnay and Pinot Noir. Denbies wines have won many national and international awards. The vineyard is open for tasting and guided tours. There is a visitors' centre in the flint-clad Chateau-style building and visitors are offered a unique insight into the wine production process. There is also a lecture room, an art gallery, a wine cellar and a restaurant.

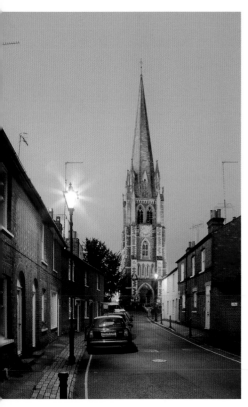

St Martin's church, Dorking.

Denbies Wine Estate near Dorking, in fog.

Denbies Hillside, Ranmore.

St Barnabas Church, Ranmore.

Ranmore Common

Ranmore Common is a sparsely populated village and an area of wooded common north-west of Dorking, on the edge of Denbies Estate. It is a site of Special Scientific Interest and the North Downs Way National Trail crosses the Common. Spectacular views from the North Downs Way and mature woodlands make it a very popular area for walkers. The parish church of St Barnabas is known not only for notable burials including Sir Harry Hylton-Foster, a former Speaker of the House of Commons, but also for its amazing architecture. This Grade II building was designed by Sir George Gilbert Scott and since it was built in 1859, remains virtually unchanged. The impressive, almost cathedral-like building and the next door school were designed in a Victorian style for over 400 workers from the Denbies Estate.

Abinger Roughs

Abinger Roughs is positioned above the village of Abinger Hammer, close to the North Downs and Pilgrims Way. The Roughs area consists of woodlands with some mature trees, open heathland and grassland. The area is maintained by the National Trust and paths are clearly marked for walkers.

Memorial cross to Samuel Wilberforce, Abinger Roughs.

Leaser's Barn, Abinger Roughs.

Bluebells near Old Simms Copse, Abinger Roughs.

There are a few car parks, one of them situated close to Leaser's Barn and Wilberforce Memorial. Samuel Wilberforce, bishop, and son of William Wilberforce, the anti-slave trade campaigner, was killed here by a fall from his horse. The Abinger Roughs is especially beautiful in the spring, when the carpet of bluebells is on display and in the autumn, when the leaves of beech trees turn golden and orange.

Westhumble

Westhumble village neighbouring Mickleham and Great Bookham was first mentioned in 1248 in the Assizes Rolls although some findings indicate that the area was occupied as long ago as the Stone

Age. The Old English name means the elm tree stump. The village first concentrated around Adlers Lane and later on around Westhumble Street which is a focus for ramblers as the Mole River Trail runs through the village. On Chapel Lane in the west end of the village there are ruins of the old 12th century chapel. This rectangular flint chapel was built for the use of the villagers, especially during the floods that made reaching Mickleham church impossible. The chapel was desecrated in the 15th century and today, only the west gable and incomplete east end remains. From 1937 it has been under the care of the National Trust and is a Scheduled Monument, listed Grade II.

Westhumble village view from Box Hill.

Norbury Park

Norbury Park is a varied landscape situated to the west of the River Mole, between Weshumble and Great Bookham. It is a working land with some tenanted farms and parkland with diverse habitats. It is popular with walkers as there are a multitude of footpaths, bridleways and cycle routes crisscrossing interesting downs, woodlands and farmlands. The park was owned by the Stydolf family and later on by the Tryon family. The next owner was William Locke, who constructed the current house away from the floodplain of the River Mole. Henry Piper, the owner in the 19th century developed the gardens and built the Weir Bridge over the River Mole, which currently is a Grade II listed bridge. Norbury Park changed hands numerous times and eventually in 1931, Surrey County Council purchased 1340 acres of the park to protect it against development. It is managed by Surrey Wildlife Trust. There are three working farms: Norbury Park, Swanworth and Bocketts Farm, the last one offering a great day out with many friendly farm animals to feed and stroke, as well as some play areas for children.

The Bookhams

Great and Little Bookham are two neighbouring villages to the south-west of Leatherhead. In the centre of Great Bookham stands St Nicholas's church, of Norman origin. It has some 11th century parts but it was enlarged in the 12th century and restored during Victorian times. Near the church there is a 15th-century tithe barn. The smaller village houses the railway station. Several of the books of the famous novelist Jane Austen were written when she stayed in Bookham. The village is however best known for Polesden Lacey National Trust house and garden. Polesden Lacey is an Edwardian house and estate located on the outskirts of Great Bookham. The extensive gardens and parkland are surrounded by breathtaking views of the Surrey Hills. The name Polesden Lacey derives from the 14th century land trader, Herbert de Polesden and later on in the same century, the owner of the place John Lacey. The very first house was built here in 1336, however it was rebuilt in the 17th century by Anthony Rous. In the 18th century the house was owned by a famous playwright Richard Brinsley Sheridan and later on, Joseph Bonsor who secured the services of Thomas Cubitt to build the neo-classical house in 1821-24. The place was much extended by Sir Ambrose Poynter in 1902-06 and later on in 1906-09 by architects Charles Mewes and Arthur Davis on the orders of the new owners, Ronald Greville and his wife, an illegitimate daughter of Edinburgh brewer, William McEwan. She was an ambitious Edwardian hostess famous for her caustic wit, and had chosen this country retreat as a perfect place to entertain royalty, writers, artists, politicians – in short, the celebrities of the time. She did it successfully for over thirty years as she manoeuvred

Polesden Lacey, Great Bookham.

well in social circles and her famed home filled with paintings, exquisite furniture, collections of porcelain and silver was favoured by the rich and famous to such an extent that even the future king, George VI and Queen Elizabeth spent their honeymoon here. Mrs Greville did not have any children and left the estate valued in today's terms at 200 million pounds to the National Trust, in memory of her father, William McEwan. The grounds extend to 12 hectares and include a walled rose garden with arched avenues, extensive lawns, winter gardens, herbaceous borders, a sunken rock garden, a lavender garden, a kitchen garden, a croquet lawn and a number of walks including the shady Nun's Walk famed for some ghostly whistling. A ghostly presence was also noted on a wooden bridge by the ornamental garden, but a long brown robe with a hood obscure the person so it is hard to say if it is the last or any of the previous owners! Behind the garden is Mrs Greville's grave as well as the dog cemetery where her much beloved dogs are buried. The estate has something interesting for all seasons and it commands some fine views of the valley, the North Downs and Ranmore.

Polesden Lacey in winter, Great Bookham.

Effingham

Effingham is a prosperous village neighbouring Great Bookham. It dates back to Saxon times and its name means "the house of Aeffing", who was a nobleman living in this area in the 5th century. In the *Domesday Book* of 1086 it was known as Epingeham. There are some interesting buildings in the village including the Red House that was designed by Edwin Lutyens. The house was built in 1893 and its garden was designed by Gertrude Jekyll. The house was converted into apartments in 2008.

Abinger Hammer

Popular with tourists and locals, Abinger Hammer is an attractive village off the A25 between Dorking and Guildford. Neighbouring villages are: Abinger Common, Sutton Abinger, Wotton and Gomshall. In the past, Abinger Hammer was recorded as Abinceborne, Abbingewurda and Abbyngere. The village is instantly recognisable by the village clock that overhangs the winding main street. "Jack the Hammer" that strikes the anvil every hour was given in memory of the first Lord Ferrer of Abinger Hall, who died in 1899. The clock is a great reminder of an iron industry flourishing in this area. The motto on the clock is: "By me you know how fast to go". The village is set beside the banks of the River Tillingbourne. The river impounded into a hammer pond in the 16th century is no longer used for the iron forging industry, but for growing watercress established in the area around the 1850s. The village green with its cricket pitch on the land given in memorial

Abinger Hammer Clock.

Abinger Hammer village green.

to the men from the village who died in the First World War is quintessentially English and is a favourite picnic place of locals and visitors. Nearby Oxmoore Copse, an Area of Outstanding Natural Beauty lies to the south of Abinger Hammer.

Wotton

Wotton village is a scattered hamlet situated in a valley at the foot of the North Downs. It stretches all the way to Friday Street. The two most significant buildings in the village are St John the Evangelist's church and Wotton House. St John's church situated at the end of Church Lane, although dating to Saxon times is mainly Victorian. Some of its interesting features are the porch door with King John and Archbishop Stephen Langton carved heads and the Evelyn Chapel with its interesting monuments including John Evelyn's tomb. John Evelyn, the diarist and garden designer was born at Wotton House in 1620. The house was the family seat of the Evelyn family and it was built in the 17th century. It was here that the very first Italian garden in England was created by John Evelyn and his brother George. The house was later extended in the 17th, 18th and 19th centuries. The house and garden are now Grade II listed. From 2003, after an extensive refurbishment, Wotton House became a hotel and conference centre run by the Principal Hayley Group.

St John's church in Wotton.

Rapeseed fields near Wotton.

Abinger Common

Abinger Common, a small village in the heart of the Surrey Hills has been called the oldest village in England. Excavations of a nearby pit-dwelling confirm that it was inhabited some 7000 years ago by Mesolithic hunters. In the village there is the 17th century Abinger Hatch Pub and the 19th century Evelyn Hall, Goddards House and St James's church. The church dates back to Norman times and is the second oldest parish church in Surrey. Badly damaged during the Second World War, it was extensively restored in 1950. Displayed outside the church is an old three person stocks. On the green, at the crossroads of the sunken lanes is Goddards House built by Edwin Lutyens in 1900 for Frederick Mirrielees. This beautiful and traditional Surrey-style house and garden laid out by Gertrude Jekyll was created as a rest and holiday home for "ladies of small means". Later on, in 1910, it was converted into a family home for Mirrielees's son, Donald. In 1991 the house was given to the Lutyens Trust and is administered by the Landmark Trust. The village is famed for its annual Medieval Fair, a tradition recreated from the past when pilgrims were given food and drink and in return, they would put on a play for the local people.

Top: *St James's churchyard, Abinger Common.*

Above: *St James's Well at Abinger Common.*

Right: *St James's Church, Abinger Common.*

Leatherhead

Leatherhead Bridge over the River Mole.

Leatherhead occupies a central location within the county of Surrey, at the northern end of the Mole Gap, a valley through which the River Mole meanders towards the River Thames. The town is of Saxon origin and to start with, it occupied the east side of the River Mole. It was a small market town named Leodridan in 880 AD, later in the 12th century, Leret, Lereda, Ledreda and Leddrede, finally settling on the name Leatherhead in the 19th century. The parish church of St Mary and St Nicholas dates from the 11th century. In 1248 Henry III granted Leatherhead a Royal Charter to host a weekly market. Good transport and a developing agricultural economy secured the growth of the town in the early centuries, whilst the coming of the railway in 1859 and several industries in the modern era enabled it to expand and modernise rapidly. Today it is a pleasant town with a pedestrianized High Street and a surprising number of shops surrounded by greenery and paths alongside the River Mole. There are many buildings of architectural and historic interest; The

Opposite: *Poppies, Westcott village.*

Running Horse dating from 1403, Wesley House, The Mansion House as well as the Sweech House and Hampton Cottage, late medieval timber-framed houses. Hampton Cottage houses a local museum famed for its collection of Ashtead Pottery. The museum also displays photographs and maps of the area and a model of the historical Leatherhead houses. St Mary and St Nicholas church was built in the 11th century but has been much altered in the 13th and later centuries. The church's medieval tower is in Perpendicular style and inside there is a 12th century chancel arch carved from chalk. Stunning countryside surrounds Leatherhead; a few minutes' walk from the centre, there is the River Mole which provides a habitat for many birds and insects. There are three listed bridges here; one of them, the amazing 14-arched bridge built in 1782 replaced an earlier medieval one. An interesting fact about the town is that Jane Austen who often visited the nearby village of Great Bookham based her fictional town of Highbury in *Emma* on Leatherhead.

Westcott

Below left: *Holy Trinity church, Westcott.*

Below right: *Westcott village green.*

Westcott lies just over a mile west of Dorking; it is a small village at the foot of the North Downs, alongside the Guildford road. The village has a few shops and an art gallery. It is busy with cyclists and walkers on their way to Leith Hill. A large green by the main road has a picturesque thatched dovecote and a bus shelter. There are some old houses in Balchins Lane, Milton Street and Westoctt Lane. The oldest of them, Stowe Marie from the 1550s, was the property of well-known actor Leslie Howard. The village saw the greatest expansion in the Victorian era. The most interesting building in the village is Holy Trinity church built by Sir George Gilbert Scott in 1852. This Grade II building has got an imposing spire with a clock.

Friday Street

Friday Street is a tiny hamlet on the west slopes of Leith Hill, a mile south of the A25. Access to it is not easy as the lanes leading to it are not only winding but narrow as well. These sunken lanes cut into the hillside, shaded by the leafy trees growing on the earth banks, lead to a hamlet set around the millpond. The area was a centre for the iron industry and hammer ponds like this one were used to power hammers to shape metal. Local pub, Stephen Langton is named in memory of a local man who later on became an Archbishop of Canterbury and a signatory of the Magna Carta. Large areas of the wooded landscape around Friday Street are owned by the National Trust.

Mill pond at Friday Street.

Holmbury St Mary village green.

Holmbury St Mary

Holmbury St Mary is a village located within Hurtwood, the largest common land in Surrey. It is nestled in a valley on the eastern slopes of Holmbury Hill. Many 19th century houses and the imposing St Mary's church give the village a largely Victorian character. The church overlooking the green was built in 1879 by George Edmund Street. The village is a good starting point for a walk to Holmbury Hill so it is popular with walkers, cyclists and horse riders. Heavily wooded Holmbury Hill is second only in height to Leith Hill and the views from there are unsurpassed. At 261 metres above sea level you can see the City of London and all the way to the sea through the Shoreham Gap. Whether this view really inspired Eric Clapton and Goerge Harrison to write "Here comes the sun" will remain uncertain. Holmbury Hill is the site of an Iron Age fort established in the 1st century AD. Excavations indicate that it was protected by double ramparts and escarpments. The area where Holmbury Hill and Pitch Hill are situated is called Hurtwood and it covers 4000 acres of forest and heathland. It is open to the public and protected by the Hurtwood Country Charitable Trust.

View from Holmbury Hill.

Peaslake

Peaslake is a small hamlet on the north slope of Hurtwood Forest. A nearby stream source called "Pise Lacu" gave the village its name. It resembles a Swiss rather than an English village due to its many chalet-style cottages perched on steep slopes. Although the area is very popular with walkers and bikers, it has managed to keep its unique small village atmosphere thanks to its remoteness and difficult access through single tracks. The main focus point in the village is the Hurtwood Inn Hotel and St Mary's church. Peaslake is surrounded by forest and nearby Pitch Hill is the fifth highest point in Surrey, at 257 metres. Plentiful rides for mountain bikes and lanes for walkers in Hurtwood Forest make the village a favourite tourist destination.

Opposite: View from Leith Hill.

Below: Leith Hill Tower on Leith Hill.

Leith Hill

Leith Hill is the highest point in South East England and is situated in beautiful wooded country, a few miles south of Dorking. At 294 metres above sea level, it is also the highest point on the greensand ridge. On top of the hill, a fortified folly was built in 1765 by Richard Hull of Leith Hill Place. From the top of the tower, sweeping views of England can be seen, as far as St Paul's Cathedral in London, the Sussex Weald, the South Downs and the English Channel to the south. On a clear day 13 counties can be seen. The next highest point to the east of Leith Hill is the Ural Mountains; they obviously cannot be seen! Leith Hill Tower is 19.5 metres high and consists of two rooms and a steep staircase leading to the top platform which is open to the public. The Hill attracts some 400,000 visitors a year. Richard Hull requested to be buried under the tower and in 1772 he was buried there in a rather unusual manner, vertically with his head facing down, as he believed that the world would be overturned on the day of judgement. Following his death, the tower fell into ruin but luckily Mr Evelyn from nearby Wotton House re-opened the tower and added the turreted side tower. Since 1923 Leith Hill and the tower are both National Trust property. The tower was fully restored in 1984 and is open most weekends. Leith Hill is home to abundant wildlife and is a Site of Special Scientific Interest. It is also interesting from a historical point of view as it was here that Ethelwulf of Wessex, father of Alfred the Great, defeated the Danes in 851. This battle was of great importance as it ended the Danes' plans to conquer England. A short distance from Leith Hill, there is Leith Hill Place, the home of Richard Hull, and later on, Josiah Wedgwood, grandson of the famous potter as well as his grandson, Ralph Vaughan Williams, the composer. The house is not open to the public, but a rhododendron wood that was created around 1900 by Caroline Wedgwood, Josiah's wife, is still there to be seen.

Christ church, Coldharbour.

Coldharbour

The village of Coldharbour nestles beneath the ancient Anstiebury Camp, now a scheduled monument. Situated north east of Leith Hill, the village is the highest community in South East England. Its name means "rough shelter for travellers" and indeed it has provided shelter since 1800 BC, at the time of the Anstiebury Camp. In spite of a mixed style of homes that are informally grouped alongside the road, the village is pleasant and quiet and many famous people settled here over the years, among them, the French painter Lucien Pissaro, the musician Ralph Vaughan Williams, the Polish poet Marian Hemar and the actor Oliver Reed.

Forest Green

The hamlet of Forest Green is situated 8 miles north of Horsham. The Holy Trinity church was built in 1897 by Charles and Christian Hensley in memory of their son Everard who was killed accidentally during rabbit shooting. This building replaced an earlier Mission Room of St. Barnabas. In the village, there are a few 15th and 16th century cottages, as well as some Victorian and Edwardian buildings along Ewhurst and Horsham Road. In the heart of the community is the Parrot Inn, which is a pub over 400 years old and is situated on the east side of the Green. Smuggler's Way between Forest Green and Leith Hill, winding and steep, was in the past as the name suggests an old contraband route, where many transactions and shipping of illegal goods took place.

Ewhurst

Ewhurst village lies on the edge of the Weald, a few miles from Cranleigh and Shere. The village takes its name from the old English, meaning "wooded hill" and "yew" suggesting that yew trees were abundant here. The village was first recorded in 1179. The parish of Ewhurst is narrow and stretches from Pitch Hill to Ellen's Green village. Pitch Hill offers spectacular views over the Weald. Much as many other villages in the medieval era, Ewhurst had lost its industrial importance by the 17th century and the local economy was supported through farming. In the 19th and the 20th century many artists and rich people moved into the area. The common land on the Weald was and still is the most densely wooded area of Britain. This area was brought to the attention of many in 1983 when the complete skeleton of an unknown dinosaur was discovered in a nearby clay pit. Displayed in the Natural History Museum it bears the name of Baryonyx Walkerii.

Ockley

Ockley is an historic village that stretches alongside the A29 road which follows the old Roman Stane Street. It was a main north-south road built between Chichester and London. The village name means "Occa's clearing in the wood", Occa being the owner of the surrounding land. The village church was built in 1291 near the place where the old Norman castle stood. Around the 16th century the village centre moved from the church's area to Stane Street. The extensive green where a village well and a pump from 1841 stands gives the feeling of spaciousness to the village. Visitors are drawn to the well-known Hannah Peschar Sculpture Garden where pieces of art are displayed in an ever changing collection. The forest garden was created by Anthony Paul and is full of broadleaved plants and mature trees.

Capel

Capel is a picturesque village positioned in the Weald near Coldharbour and Beare Green, only a few miles from the bustling town of Dorking. The original settlement consisted of a few farms. The chapel of ease that was built here gave the village the name. Agriculture and farming played an important role in the village in the early centuries but from the 17th century until the present day, brick making became an important source of income for the village. In the 17th and the 18th century the house of the Bax family became an active centre for a Quaker Community and today this meeting house is a listed building. The local chapel was upgraded to a parish church in 1334 and dedicated to St Lawrence. In the 16th century the name was changed to St John the Baptist. The eclectic mix of houses creates a quaint village and extensive farms with open countryside make this area a favourite with walkers.

Scott's Well, village green, Ockley.

Newdigate

Newdigate village lies midway between Dorking, Reigate and Horsham. The name derives from "on Ewood gate". The neighbouring villages include Capel and Charlwood. The prosperity of the village is linked with the ironwork industry that lasted here until the early 17th century. With the arrival of the railway to nearby Holmwood, the area became popular with commuters. St Peter's church, a Grade II listed building dates back to the 12th century. Its tower is a unique example of an oak building. Amidst many old timber houses, the oldest are: Tanhouse from 1540, Nyes Place from 1575 and Reffolds from 1606.

Burford Bridge Hotel, Mickleham.

Mickleham

A sleepy village called Mickleham stands on the old Roman Road known as Stane Street, by the River Mole, one mile from Box Hill. At the heart of the village is the ancient St Michael's church with a Norman tower and a chancel arch. There are a few quintessentially English pubs in the village. Burford Bridge Hotel on the edge of the village's claim to fame is that Lord Nelson stayed here a few times. The River Mole is a tributary of the River Thames. It starts its journey in West Sussex, not far from Gatwick Airport and flows through Surrey all the way to Hampton Court where it merges into the River Ember, where they both enter the Thames. The very first time this river was recorded was in 983 under the name of Emen. In the medieval period the name changed into Amele and Emele and only in the 16th century was the name was changed to Mole. Mola in Latin means a mill and there were many mills built alongside the river. In fact, in as early as 1086 there were over 20 mills. The river gives its name to the Mole valley, a rich habitat of scrubs, woodland, hedges, meadows and river. It is home to many animals, birds, insects and fish. The River Mole is famed for its large diversity of fish, chub, barbell, trout and many more varieties. Twelve Sites of Special Scientific Interest are within the Mole catchment area. Mole Gap is a break in the North Downs and is situated just below Box Hill. Stepping stones at the crossing point were rebuilt here after the war and dedicated to Prime Minister Clement Attlee. This part of the river, with open vistas on the North Downs Way and spectacular 170-metres river cliff, is popular with walkers. The River Mole is famous for its swallow holes: several curious hollows created by the river. The river flowing underground creates sinkholes in the soft chalk by thinning the ground and collapsing. There are over twenty five smaller holes and a few large ones. Some of them were covered by concrete domes with an access for maintenance. The disappearing of the water below the ground created many stories and legends. Unlike the River Wey, the River Mole in spite of a few attempts to make it navigational, was never really used for navigation due to lack of funds. During World War II the banks of the river were fortified in many locations with pill boxes, gun mounts and anti-tank cubes to create a defensive line protecting London.

Stepping stones on the River Mole at the foot of Box Hill.

Box Hill

Box Hill stands at the south eastern corner of the Mole Gap. It is famous for the panoramic views and since the arrival of the railway to Dorking, it has been a popular tourist attraction. The name comes from the ancient box trees growing on the slopes of the summit; some of them are over a thousand years old. There are some historical Bronze Age burial mounds here and a Roman Road lies at the bottom of the hill, near Mickleham Downs. Some 13th century documents mention this hill as Atteboxe or Buxeto, both names that are connected with box trees. Salomons Memorial viewpoint offers spectacular vistas towards East and West Sussex, with Chanctonbury Ring and Devil's Dyke visible on a good day. It has been built to commemorate Leopold Salomons, who gave 230 acres of Box Hill to the National Trust. It is not however the highest point of Box Hill. The Highest point is Betchworth Clumps at 224 metres, which is situated close to the Hand-in-Hand pub. The gentler slope on the side of Burford Spur offers beautiful open chalk countryside, while the steep zig-zag valley is favoured by cyclists. It was here that the Olympic Cycling Road Races of 2012 took place. Box Hill is a Special Area of Conservation with rare species of flora and fauna, including over a dozen species of rare orchids, forty species of butterflies and thirteen species of bats. The Hill has also some of the most ancient woodlands in Britain, with box trees characterised by their twisted trunks and gnarled branches, and beech trees with vivid red and orange leaves in the autumn. A small flock of sheep and cattle help clear the scrubland of Box Hill, maintaining the chalk downlands habitat and preventing it becoming woodland. The Hill is famed for its natural beauty but it is also home to two interesting man-made structures, the Old Fort and the Broadway Folly. The Victorian fort standing on the summit was built in the late 1890s and was one of 13 mobilisation centres designed to help in the defence of London. Decommissioned in 1908, it can still be admired from the outside; inside the fort is a precious bat habitat. Close to the fort, on the edge of the slope stands a cross marking the place where Major Peter Labelliere, a well-loved eccentric from Dorking was buried upside down. The top of the hill was his favourite place to meditate and it was his wish to be buried here in this extraordinary way, as he claimed that the world was "topsy-turvey". Broadwood Folly situated on the northern tip of Lodge Hill is a ruined flint tower overlooking the Juniper Hall in Mickleham. It was built for Thomas Broadwood, the owner of Juniper Hall. The holm oak growing inside the tower shows the determination of nature to reclaim the place. Box Hill's tranquil and peaceful summit is a coveted place of outstanding natural beauty visited by almost one million people a year. So much loved by Victorian day trippers, it is increasingly popular with cyclists, and walkers. The National Trust café on the top offers refreshments to all.

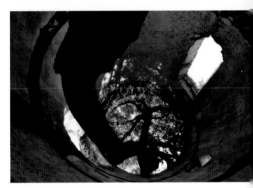

Broadwood Folly, Box Hill.

Opposite: *Zig zag road at Box Hill.*

Sunrise at Box Hill.

Chapter 4

Around Reigate

Reigate

REIGATE IS A prosperous residential town and the history of Reigate can be traced back to the times of William the Conqueror. The King awarded the land at the foot of the North Downs to his knight, William de Warenne. His son, William de Warenne II built Reigate Castle here. Later on, around 1150, the Earl de Warenne laid out a new town below the castle, which replaced the nearby settlement of Cherchefelle. The new name, Reigate, comes most probably from the deer park gate. Some traces of earlier settlement indicate that the area was occupied in Neolithic, Bronze Age as well as in Roman times. As the de Warennes were absentee landlords due to the fact that they had properties in Sussex, Yorkshire and Normandy, the castle deteriorated quickly. During the 17th century, whatever was left of the castle was demolished and only some earthworks are left today and protected as a scheduled monument. Although the castle has gone, the grounds were turned into a nice park. The Gatehouse that is situated in a prominent place in the gardens was built in 1777 from the castle stones by Richard Barnes in memory of William de Warenne. Underneath the castle and the town are some caves. The history of the caves is not clear, but most probably they are the remains of some salt mines and dungeons that in later centuries were used as storage spaces for shops. The steep path from the castle grounds leads to the town centre. An attractive mixture of Victorian and Georgian buildings is concentrated on and around High Street and Bell Street. This part of the town was in existence in the 12th and the 13th centuries. Today a large part of it has been designated as a Conservation Area of Special Historic Interest. The present Town Hall was built in 1901 and is a listed building, whilst the Old Town Hall was built in 1708 and still stands in the heart of the town, although today not any more the Town Hall, but a restaurant. Other noteworthy buildings are: the timber-framed La Trobes home on the High Street, Old Sweep's House on Slipshoe Street and St Mary's church in Chart Lane. St Mary's church is not only the resting place of Lord Howard of Effingham, a close friend of Francis Drake and Sir Walter Raleigh but also home to Cranston Library. It was the first lending library in England. Among some two thousand books are some precious manuscripts like the 14th-century book written by Stephen Byrchington and Lord Howard's prayer book from 1566.

Opposite: *Inglis Folly, Colley Hill, Reigate.*

Reigate Church Mill, Reigate.

View from Reigate Heath.

Reigate Heath, Reigate.

Reigate Fort, Reigate.

Reigate Castle grounds, Reigate.

Reigate expanded rapidly after 1841 with the coming of the railway. An important part in the history of Reigate was played by the Priory. Founded in the early 13th century for Regular Canons of the Order of St Augustine, it was closed in 1535 and granted to Lord Howard of Effingham by Henry VIII after the Dissolution of the Monasteries. The Priory was converted into a residence for the Howard family. Later on in 1681, London brewer, John Parsons bought the property. Over the years it was remodelled and today it is a Palladian mansion with some fine period features. It houses Reigate Priory Museum and Reigate Priory School. It is surrounded by 65 acres of open parkland with extensive playing fields, a skate-park, woodlands and a picturesque pond.

Reigate has got two windmills: to the north a tower mill, Wray Mill at Wray Common; and a post mill at Reigate Heath, to the west of the town. The windmill at Reigate Heath is unique as it is also a church. It is the only windmill in England that has been converted into a church. North of Reigate lies Reigate Hill (220 m) and Colley Hill (230 m). Both hills offer spectacular views from the top. From the early 20th century land here was acquired and donated to the National Trust. On top of Colley Hill there is the "Inglis Folly". Donated in 1909, this round structure was originally a drinking

Reigate Priory Pond, Reigate.

Reigate Priory Museum, Reigate.

fountain for horses but was later replaced by a directions indicator pointing to many Surrey Hills towns. The ceiling of the memorial is highly decorated, representing the heavens.

Sitting on top of Reigate Hill is the 19th century Reigate Fort. It was part of a series of mobilisation centres built between 1890 and 1903. Thirteen such centres alongside the London defensive line were constructed to protect London from invasion from the south coast. All forts varied in design but their main role was to store tools and ammunition as well as act as strong points. Reigate Fort was aligned east-west and is surrounded by a rampart and a ditch. The subterranean magazine block consists of two chambers. The fort however played another military role during the Second World War, when it was re-commissioned and used by the Canadian Army. It was also here that the South East Command led by Lieutenant General Montgomery was based in caves next to the fort. Reigate Fort has been owned by the National Trust since 1932. In 1972 it was designated as a Scheduled Ancient Monument and in 2000 it was restored. In 2007 it opened its door to the public and is a popular attraction showing many original features including casemates, ramparts, firing platforms and tool stores.

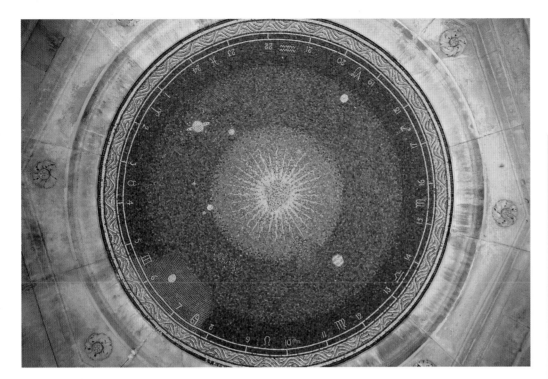

Ceiling of the Inglis Memorial in
Colley Hill, Reigate

Reigate Wray Mill.

Inglis Memorial, Colley Hill,
Reigate.

Colley Hill, Reigate.

Buckland

Buckland is an attractive village situated between Dorking and Reigate. Sitting on a ridge of land where the A25 turns south-west, a large part of the village is a Conservation Area. It is home to 26 listed buildings. The village is bordered by the North Downs escarpment and surrounded by many farms that belong to the Dungates Estate. The current owner family bought Buckland Estate in 1635. Apart from managing the farms, the Estate also leases the mineral rights for sand extraction. The village appeared in *Domesday Book* when it was posessed by John of Tonbridge, who owned at the

Buckland village green.

time a significant part of Surrey. Today the village's main tourist attractions are the church of St Mary the Virgin and the three village greens; the one with the pond is one of the most photographed. St Mary the Virgin church is the only church in the village and is positioned opposite the green with the pond. The present church was built in 1380 although the first mention of the church was recorded in 1086. During the 1860s the church underwent a significant refurbishment by Henry Woodyer who was praised for his work – the church is considered as "Victorian church building at its best". There are some copies of the 14th century stained glass windows here, considered to be the finest example of such work in Surrey. The bell tower's internal structure is 14th century, with pews and panelling from the 17th century. The village's Shag Brook according to local legend was home to a monstrous horse dragging travellers to a boulder in the middle of the brook. Such terror did this legend instil in local people and travellers that parson Willoughby Bertie removed the stone and threw it off Devon Cliff in 1757. There is also a windmill in the village, regrettably hidden from the public view. The windmill was built in 1860 and worked no more than thirty years. It is a very rare type of mill, a small wind-powered sawmill, the only one of this kind in England. It was rediscovered in 1995 and restored through the years 1995-2004.

Betchworth

St Michael's church, Betchworth.

Betchworth village is situated on the main Reigate-Dorking Road, 3 miles west of Reigate. The village, nicely positioned by the River Mole appeared in the *Domesday Book*. Originally a small cluster of buildings around St Michael's church, the village grew when the railway arrived here. Some interesting buildings are: the 16th century-Old Mill Cottage, Georgian manor Betchworth House, the 18th century vicarage as well as many 17th and 18th century cottages. The church of St Michael has stood in the village for over 900 years. Today there are only some traces of the Saxon church, like the stone in the tower's south window. The north windows are Norman. Two major alterations took place here – in 1851 when the old crossing tower was demolished and in 1879 when the north transept was built. Inside the church two fascinating items are the map of the local manor from 1634 and a pre-Norman wooden chest made from a single piece of oak. Many prominent people lived in Betchworth. Thomas Morsted, the surgeon to Henry IV and Henry V, lived with his parents at More Place and bequeathed money to the church. Sir Benjamin Collins Brodie, surgeon to Queen Victoria, lived at Broome Park. St Michael's church has many interesting brasses and memorials to many of the eminent parishioners. A very interesting, though little known, building is Betchworth Castle situated a couple of miles west of the village, by the River Mole. The ruin of this fortified medieval house can only be viewed with prior permission, due to its dangerous state. The castle was built in the 11th century by Robert Fitz Gilbert. In 1379 Sir John Fitzalan turned it into a stone castellated house.

Forge, Betchworth.

In the 15th century the castle underwent further changes on the orders of Sir Thomas Browne. The castle fell into disrepair, part of it was dismantled and in the 19th century it became a romantic ruin, supposedly haunted by the ghost of Lord Hope wringing his hands in despair as by mistake he had killed his own son. The castle was sold in 2008 to Martin Higgins, a local historic building enthusiast who plans to repair the castle, clear the paths and improve the landscape.

Brockham

The flourishing village of Brockham stands on the River Mole, south of Boxhill, with the North Downs as a picturesque backdrop. Originally called Brookham, it was a small hamlet in the possession of the de Warenne family until the 17th century. The name of the village underwent many distortions and since 1800 the modern version has been used. Surrounded by farmland, the village inhabitants are mainly employed in agriculture and also in brick manufacture as the area is rich in clay and sand. The original historic buildings with timber framing and some with thatched roofs surround a triangular village green with an imposing parish church. The land for the church was a gift

from Mr Hope of Depedene, who bought the manor here in 1844. Christ Church was commissioned by Sir Henry Gouldburn and designed by Benjamin Ferrey, an associate of Augustus Pugin, who designed interiors in the Palace of Westminster. The church is an imposing stone building with the tower and spire seen for miles. The village grew rapidly in the 1920s and 1930s, when two roads, the A24 and the A25, were improved and it enabled the village to become a fashionable commuter's area. The village green is popular for cricket matches and it is also well known also for its large Guy Fawkes Bonfire Night. The celebration attracts some twenty thousand people and its fireworks display can be seen from Box Hill.

Christ Church, Brockham.

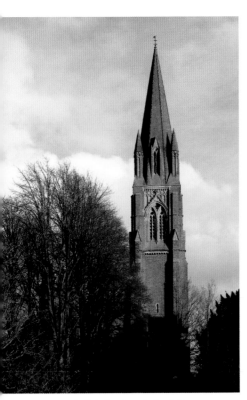

St John's church Redhill.

Redhill

Redhill is situated to the south of the North Downs. Unlike its neighbouring town of Reigate, it doesn't have a long history. Originally a hamlet in the area around Warwick Road, it became known as Warwick Town. It was transformed into a Victorian railway town around 1841 with the arrival of the railway from London to Brighton. The railway provided an opportunity for commuters and the town underwent rapid growth. Most of the town's buildings date from this period. The name changed from Warwick Town to Redhill as the post office established in Red Hill Common area was moved to Station Road but its stamp "Red Hill" stayed and all the letters were stamped as Redhill, not Warwick Town; the old name fell into disuse and Redhill as a name was officially taken in 1856. Redhill quickly became the area's commercial centre; however development was halted by the Second World War. In the years from 1950 to 1980, the town underwent a massive modernisation and revitalisation. Today its High Street is pedestrianized and there are two large shopping centres, the Belfry Shopping Centre as well as Warwick Quadrant. Redhill has its own aerodrome, which is situated to the south-east of the town. It was opened in 1933 on the area of Hamme Farm.

Redhill High Street.

Originally it was only used for private flying by the Redhill Flying Club. Later on, it became used as an alternative airport to Croydon by Imperial Airways and an RAF station in the Second World War. In the 1950s and 1960s it again restarted club flying as well as helicopter training. The new terminal building and control tower were added in 1986 and in 1991. The aerodrome was bought by Redhill Aerodrome Ventures Ltd. Today it operates pleasure flights, private commercial flights and various flying courses. Over the years, many famous people lived and visited Redhill. Perhaps the most famous guest here was Swedish chemist Alfred Nobel who demonstrated for the first time at the local quarry in 1867 his new explosive, dynamite. A few years earlier, Richard Carrington, an astronomer, made an important observation here about solar flares and their influence upon the Earth. Today Redhill is a busy commuter town with some green areas such as Redhill Common, Gatton Park and Earlswood Lakes nearby.

Charlwood

Charlwood is a pretty village immediately north-west of Gatwick Airport, on the eastern edge of the Surrey Hills. There are over 80 historic 15th to 18th century fine cottages that were built as a result of a prosperous ironworking industry in the Middle Ages. The Bristow Cottage was the school building from 1620 to 1852; the Cage that was a village lock up, dates from 1792. Most of the older houses are hidden in smaller lanes. The parish church of St Nicholas dates to 1080. The most interesting features of the church are its Norman framework, the 13th century wall paintings, stained glass windows and wooden roof beams. A chantry chapel was added in 1480. Charlwood is home of Lowfield Heath Windmill which was re-erected on the edge of the village in 1989. The mill was in continuous work until 1899 and again after careful restoration, in 1989. Charlwood village is surrounded by farmlands and woodlands; two of the nearby woodlands, Glovers Wood and Edolph's Copse are managed by the Woodland Trust and famed for their bluebell display in the spring.

Gatton Park

Situated at the foot of the North Downs, near Reigate, is Gatton Park, a 600 acres estate with 260 acres of historic parkland. The park at Gatton is Surrey's hidden treasure that was designed by Lancelot "Capability" Brown in the years 1762-1766. The Gatton Trust manages all 260 acres of parkland, while the rest of the estate is owned by the National Trust. Gatton Park, a Grade II listed Palladian-style mansion is owned by the Royal Alexandra and Albert School, a voluntary assisted boarding and day school. It offers some spectacular views to the south over the parterre and the

Gatton Park Country Estate.

Opposite: *Gatton Park,
view to the lake.*

St Andrew's church, Gatton Park.

row of elegant cast stone urns, towards parklands and the main lake. The mansion changed hands many times. In the 17th century it was owned by John Weston of Sutton Place. It was acquired in 1748 by James Colebrooke and it was his brother, George, who employed Capability Brown to transform the existing formal landscape into a much-loved natural English-style parkland with dramatic vistas, large lake, serpentine canals, cascades and smaller ponds. Before Gatton Park was turned into the Royal Alexandra and Albert School, two more owners greatly improved the estate: Frederick John Monson, 5th Baron Monson from 1830 and Sir Jeremiah Colman from 1888. The latter made many alternations and additions to the estate and gardens. He was an avid gardener with a passion for orchids and was so successful that some of the species were sent as far as New Zealand and Ceylon. The Japanese Garden beside the Engine Pond constructed in 1909 for Jeremiah Colman was lost until the 1950s when it was restored by the Gatton Trust. Today, the thatched tea-house, bridge and paths look exactly like the original garden and some surviving plants as well as

Above left: *Hop Garden Pond, Gatton Park.*

Above right: *Gatton Park Country Estate.*

new ones perfectly encapsulate the spirit of this Eastern paradise. The rock and water gardens are the Edwardian pleasure gardens. Ordered by Jeremiah Colman and constructed by Pulham & Sons in 1912, they were so dramatic that Queen Mary visited the place frequently. An artificial Pulhamite rock blended perfectly with natural rock, while the sloping lawn and the pond added interest to the gardens that were planted carefully with alpine and aquatic plants. The gardens are stunningly beautiful in February with a display of snowdrops and aconites. Beyond the parkland, there are mixed woodlands; Temple Wood consists of ash, hazel, oak, beech and yew trees; Serpentine Wood has ash, beech and poplar; Tower Wood is predominantly made up of beech and yew. Next to Gatton Hall there is St Andrew's church dating to the 16th century. It was restored in 1834 by E. Webb architect for the 5th Lord Monson. The Gatton Trust staff and volunteers promote the park for education and enjoyment and it is open on the first Sunday of each month from February through to October.

Nutfield

Nutfield village mentioned in the *Domesday Book* as Notfelle is situated on the ridge between Redhill and Bletchingley. The main attractions of the village are St Peter's and St Paul's church where there is an altar tomb of Edmandus Molyneux, Nutfield Priory Hotel, Priory Farm and nearby Mercer's Country Park. Nutfield Priory is a country mansion set on Nutfield Ridge. The original mansion was built here in 1849-54 but it was demolished by new owner, Joshua Fielden. His newly built mansion was inspired by Neo-Gothic design. The architect, John Gibson based his design on the Palace of Westminster. Despite the name, it was never a priory – the name comes from the land it stands on, the Prior's Land. In 1930 the mansion was turned into a country house hotel. Priory Farm just below Nutfield Priory was a traditional working farm until 1992. The farmland was used to grow wheat and barley; later on a "pick your own" business was started here and a farm shop with bedding plants was opened. Diversification was the key and today it still adjusts to demands and needs. New businesses that have been set up here are mountain boarding, fishing, as well as a Discovery Walk with pathways alongside some stunning plantations.

Mercer's Country Park off Nutfield Marsh Road was established in a former quarry pit. As well as a circular walk around the lake there is a large range of water sports taking place here. The area is a well-established bird reserve with moorhens, lapwings, skylarks, snipes, as well as many ducks and other waders.

Nutfield Priory.

St Mary the Virgin church, Bletchingley.

Bletchingley

Bletchingley village is sandwiched between Godstone and Redhill and is of medieval origin. The village lies on the greensand ridge. Within a walking distance of the village there lies the North Downs and Greensand Way. Although Roman activity has been recorded in the area, Bletchingley dates back to Saxon times. Recorded in the *Domesday Book* as Blachingelei, it belonged to Richard de Tonebridge. The village's medieval character is still visible today; the Whyte Harte Inn is one of the oldest pubs in Britain and it dates to 1388. St Mary's church has a typically squat, 12th-century tower. There was a spire until lightning destroyed it in 1606. Inside the church there is a 13th-century hermit's cell, a monument to Sir Robert Clayton, Lord Mayor of London, as well as the impressive tomb of Thomas Cawarden, owner of Bletchingley Place Manor. Bletchingley Place was given to Anne of Cleves who lived here after her marriage to Henry VIII was annulled. There are also some other historic buildings on the High Street. Sadly Bletchingley Castle built in 1160 was almost completely demolished in 1264 and only some earthworks are visible today. St Mary's church's oldest part is the tower, which was built in 1090. The porch and the great oak door as well as the chancel arch date from 1460. Many influential people lived in the village over the centuries and there are some interesting memorials and effigies in the church. Period houses, cottages and Georgian villas line the High Street, together with some antique shops and five old pubs that all give the village a quintessentially English look.

Godstone

Godstone village was initially known as Wachelestede and Walingstead. The name Godstone appeared in 1248 and it was derived from Goda's Tun, Goda being the daughter of King Ethelred II who had land in this area and built the first church here. The village was built on the old Roman road and consists of two centres, Church Town and Godstone Green. The first centre, quiet and secluded, grew upon the high ground around the medieval church. To the south of the church a group of alms houses and a chapel were built by Sir George Gilbert Scott in 1872 on the request of

Godstone.

Overleaf: *Harvest near Godstone.*

Mrs Mabel Hunt, in memory of her only daughter who died very young. Godstone Green lies along the main road, half a mile to the west of the church and is framed by historic buildings. Today the village green boasts a very picturesque pond, some football pitches and a cricket pitch. Cricket has been played here since 1749. The official Godstone Cricket Club was founded in 1868 and is still going strong today. The pond at Godstone Green was used by wagoners as a horse pond. The other village pond, the Bay Pond, is within a walking distance from the green on the path to the church. Godstone's Tudor and Elizabethan character survived intact. There is a selection of historic country inns, The Rose and Crown, Hare and Hounds and the White Hart. The White Hart was a stopping place used by Queen Elizabeth I, Queen Victoria and the Tsar of Russia. The Hare and Hounds pub, as legend has it, was the place where famous pirate and smuggler, John Edward Trenchman died of wounds after he was ambushed at Tilburstow Hill. The villagers buried him in an unmarked grave and that must have upset him, as he started to haunt the graveyard. The frightening things continued in and around St Nicholas's church until the pirate's body was reburied, with a full service and a proper headstone was erected next to the church. The church is Norman in origin but it was extensively rebuilt by Sir George Gilbert Scott in 1872-73, one of the leading architects of the Victorian era. Godstone's most important industry was stone quarrying that left a labyrinth of tunnels, caves and galleries in the North Downs. Other industries established here were sand and gravel quarries, and digging and processing iron ore. There were also some mills producing gunpowder.

Oxted

Oxted village or as it was known earlier Acstede meaning "a place where oaks grew" lies on the slope of the hill, 3 miles east of Godstone. Old Oxted is concentrated around High Street while the New Town developed further away, near the train station of the railway line opened in 1884. Oxted stayed in the hands of Roland of Oxted until mid-14th century; later on it was owned by Robert de Stangrave, Sir Reginald Cobham, John Reed and since 1587 by the Hoskins family. Positioned just below the Downs, it had good trading links with the whole of the Surrey area making it a prosperous village. Many timber-framed 15th to 17th century houses survived in this charming village. St Mary's church positioned on the prominent mound to the north-east of the village, has many Norman features. It is a bit of a mystery whether the mound is natural or if it was created in Norman times. Perhaps the most interesting fact about the village is that it is situated exactly on the Greenwich Meridian at zero degrees of longitude. Two prominent people lived in the village: Harold Darke (1888-1976) who composed the music to popular Christmas carol "In the Bleak Midwinter", and the writer Joseph Conrad (1857-1924), of Polish origin, precursor of modernist literature.

Titsey Place

Titsey Place is one of the largest surviving historical estates nestling under the North Downs. It dates back to the mid-16th century when it was bought by Sir John Gresham. There is a magnificent manor house, spectacular gardens including walled kitchen gardens, landscaped lakes, rose garden as well as extensive parkland and woodland. Prominent merchant of Tudor Period, John Gresham bought the manors of Titsey, Tatsfield, Westerham, Lingfield and Sanderstead in 1534. This talented man was Lord Mayor of London, member of the Mercer's Livery Company and was trading with the Middle East, Baltic countries and Russia. Respected by Queen Elizabeth I, he was knighted in 1547. His son, William, inherited Titsey and improved the estate significantly. He also built a new home here. Unfortunately hardly anything is left of the house, as it was demolished in the 18th century. During the Parliamentarian's rule, the house was confiscated but returned to the Gresham family at the restoration of Charles II in 1660. By 1742 the estate was in serious trouble as Marmaduke Gresham spent the family's fortune and left the manor in ruin. His son, John, on inheriting the property married an heiress and was lucky enough to inherit a fortune from his uncle that allowed him to demolish the old manor and build here a lovely Georgian house. Sir John Gresham's daughter, Katherine Maria was the last of the Gresham family; she married William Gower and the house stayed in their hands. Granville Leveson Gower was responsible for significant remodelling of the house and establishing the gardens of Titsey Place. He was also an avid historian and archaeologist and to the south of the house he excavated two Roman sites in 1867. His two grandsons, Richard and Thomas were bachelors and

Titsey Place gardens.

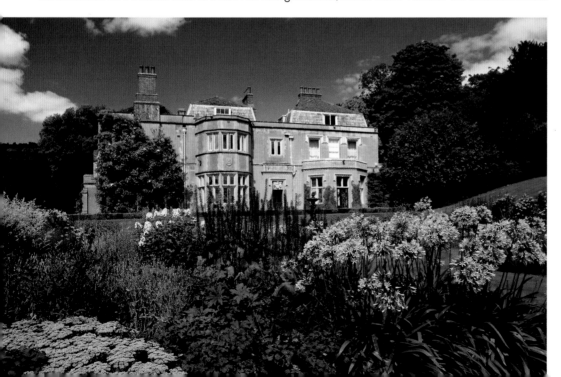

Titsey Place.

as they had no close relations, they formed the Titsey Foundation with an aim of preserving the house and gardens and opening the estate to the public. In 1993 the manor house and gardens were opened to the public and they can be visited during the summer months. The house was designed by William Atkinson and features an oak panelled sitting room, the Old Hall and the gallery bedroom. It houses porcelain collections, exquisite furniture, a large collection of family portraits and a set of four Canaletto pictures of Venice. The grounds include the lakes fed from a chalybeate spring, a waterfall, stone bridge, fountain, island on the lake, temples, rose garden, terraces with long views over the parkland, dovecote, old diary, ornamental farm buildings, and a conservatory full of exotic plants. Some 500 acres of woodland are open to the public most of the year with two main routes around the plantations. The estate is quintessentially English with rolling hills and woodland in the background. St James's church situated on the other side of Titsey Road was moved there by Sir John Gresham in 1776; the old site is marked by a one-thousand-year-old yew tree.

Titsey Place gardens.
Opposite: Titsey Place.

Limpsfield

The village of Limpsfield appeared in the *Domesday Book* in 1086 as Limenesfeld. It is located near Oxted village and Titsey Estate, in the shadow of the North Downs. The main part of the village is a conservation area with many interesting buildings alongside High Street. Three well known rights of way, the Pilgrim's Way, Greensand Way and Vanguard Way are on the village's doorstep. Limpsfield Common used from the 14th century by commoners for grazing animals and collecting wood is now managed by the National Trust. From 1934 it was managed by a committee set up by a local squire and residents. It is a combination of heathland, grassland and woodlands. Today it is mainly used for recreational activities. In the parish church of St Peter the oldest part dates from about 1180, however it was extensively restored in the 19th century. In the churchyard, the composer Frederick Delius and conductor Sir Thomas Beecham are buried. Two very old buildings in the village are an imposing Grade II Victorian school for the children of missionaries, currently converted into apartments and, much older, the Old Court Cottage in Titsey Road, a Grade I listed building from 1190. Despite some later alterations in the 14th and 16th century, it is still a perfect example of a timber frame building from the 12th century.

Yew tree in the churchyard of St George's church, Crowhurst.

Crowhurst

Possibly the most interesting attraction of Crowhurst village is a massive hollow yew tree standing in St George's churchyard. A tree thought to be four thousand years old, it is possibly the oldest yew tree in the country. Its swirly pink bark, as some people believe, depicts the face of an old man.

The trunk is hollow and the wooden door has been built into the tree sometime after 1820. It is believed that the tree was used at certain times as a summer house. During the Civil War, a large cannon ball was fired and later on discovered embedded in it.

Outwood

Outwood village is home to the oldest working mill in England. The mill was built in 1665 for Thomas Budgen. It is a post mill of a turret type on a single storey roundhouse. The body of a post mill with the machinery rotates around a central post. The mill is almost 12 metres, five storeys high which makes it the tallest smock mill ever built. The mill has four spring sails and drives two pairs of millstones. Over the years the mill carried many sails and was equipped with a clever feature allowing the angle of the sails to be adjusted to wind conditions. The mill was grinding corn and producing flour until 2012 when the sails were unfortunately significantly damaged during a very bad storm. In the 18th century yet another smock mill was built next to this one but was quickly closed and eventually collapsed. The Outwood Mill was owned by the Jupp family from 1806 until 1962 and later on by G & R Thomas.

Burstow

The village of Burstow lies 7 miles south east of Reigate. In the heart of the village is St Bartholomew, a half-timbered, 11th century church. Buried in the church is John Flamsted, rector of Burstow and King Charles II's Astronomer Royal, whose detailed measurements of star positions made navigation safe.

Lingfield

Lingfield is a large village in the south-east of Surrey. Set within wooded countryside it sits between the tributaries of Eden Brook. It was recorded for the first time in the 9th century as Leangafeld. The village, originally attached to the Abbey, in the 14th century was in the hands of de Cobham family. Sir Reginald Cobham founded here in 1431 a College for Secular Chaplains. Unfortunately the only part of the building that survived is the Old Guest House of the College, which today is occupied by the local library. Very little remains also from Starborough Castle fortified by Lord Cobham; it was dismantled by Parliamentary forces in 1648 and only the moat survived, which today is filled with water. The village has many timber-framed buildings from the 15th to the 17th centuries. One part of

Lingfield Cage

the village has developed around St Peter and St Paul's church, while the other one is near the Old Cage and St Peter's Cross from the 15th century. The Old Cage was used as a jail for minor offenders from 1773 until 1882. Next to it there is a hollow oak tree that is four hundred years old. There has been a church in the village since Saxon times, but only part of the walls from this time exists in today's St Peter and St Paul's church. This church is the only large church in Perpendicular style in Surrey – it is so large that is called the "Westminster Abbey" of the South East. Rebuilt in 1431 by Sir Reginald Cobham it is famous for the vast collection of brasses and monuments. The impressive tomb of Reginald Cobham and his family resting place is in the north aisle. There is also a very old font from the 15th century and some interesting Victorian stained-glass windows. The most interesting buildings in the town are positioned on Broad Street, down from the church and include the 15th century Pollard Cottage, 16th century Old Town Stores and the 18th century Star Inn Cottage.

Haxted Watermill.

Lingfield is famous for its racecourse which was opened in 1890. It stages racing throughout the year. Near the village, Haxted Mill can be found; this double fronted mill was built in two halves, the first in 1580 and the second one in 1794. It is powered by the River Eden and was mentioned in the will of Sir Reginald de Cobham in 1361. It is restored and inside there is water-powered machinery on display. Another nearby attraction is the British Wildlife Centre in Newchapel. It was started in 1997 by David Mills on the site of a former dairy farm. The main aim of the centre is to educate visitors about native wildlife, to help them to understand the behaviour of animals and to see the animals in their natural habitat. The Centre features different habitats from grasslands through forest, ponds to hedgerows. It has a fine collection of over 40 species: deer, foxes, pine martens, Scottish wildcats and many birds of prey as well as amphibians, reptiles and fish. The Centre features wetland boardwalks, a walk through open air enclosures, pens, walkways, clear fronted tunnels and viewing chambers.

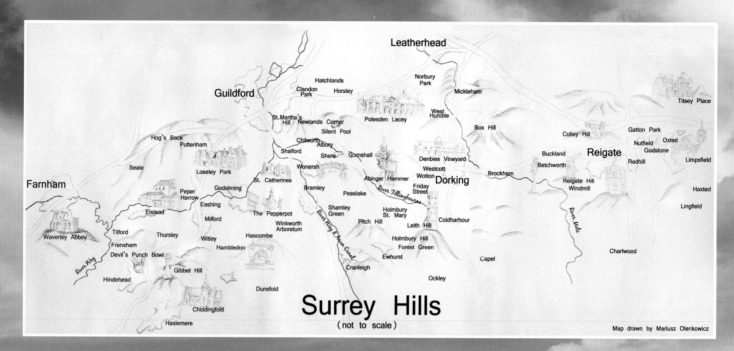

Surrey Hills

(not to scale)

Leatherhead

Guildford

Farnham

Hatchlands
Clandon Park
Horsley
Norbury Park
Mickleham

St.Martha's Hill
Newlands Corner
Silent Pool
Polesden Lacey
West Humble
Box Hill

Hog's Back
Puttenham
Chilworth
Albury
Shalford
Shere
Gomshall
Colley Hill
Gatton Park
Titsey Place

Seale
Loseley Park
Wonersh
Denbies Vineyard
Westcott
Wotton
Dorking
Buckland
Betchworth
Reigate
Nutfield
Oxted
Godstone

St. Catherines
Bramley
Abinger Hammer
Friday Street
Brockham
Redhill
Limpsfield

Peper Harrow
Godalming
Peaslake
Holmbury St. Mary
Coldharbour
Reigate Hill Windmill
Haxted

Elstead
Eashing
Milford
The Pepperpot
Winkworth Arboretum
Shamley Green
Pitch Hill
Leith Hill
Lingfield

Waverley Abbey
Tilford
Thursley
Witley
Hascombe
Holmbury Hill
Forest Green
Charlwood

Frensham
Devil's Punch Bowl
Hambledon
Ewhurst
Capel

Hindehead
Gibbet Hill
Cranleigh
Ockley

Chiddingfold
Dunsfold

Haslemere

River Way
River Tillingbourne
River Wey & Arun Canal
River Mole

Map drawn by Mariusz Olenkowicz

Surrey Hills Places of Interest

The Brooking Collection
44 The Drive, Cranleigh, tel: 01483 274202
The Brooking Collection of Architectural Details is the only major national collection of its kind in the UK. It charts the evolution of British building over the period of the last 500 years. Founder, Charles Brooking, has rescued architectural features from national landmark buildings, terrace houses, country estates and cottages since 1966.

Clandon Park
West Clandon, Guildford, Surrey, GU4 7RQ, tel: 01483 222482
Palladian mansion with grand marble hall and porcelain collection, as well as attractive gardens containing a parterre, grotto, sunken Dutch garden and a Maori house.

Craft Study Centre
University College for the Creative Arts at Farnham, Falkner Road, Farnham, Surrey, GU9 7DS tel: 01252 891450
The Craft Study Centre is a charity created by artist-makers and educators to protect the best of modern British crafts. Home to a collection of modern and contemporary craft, it displays modern and contemporary calligraphy, ceramics, textiles, furniture and wood as well as maker's diaries, working notes, and photographs dating from the 1920s.

Dorking Museum and Heritage Centre
The Old Foundry, 62 West Street, Dorking, Surrey, RH4 1BS
tel: 01306 876591
Dorking Museum presents the story of Dorking, the surrounding villages, the landscape and local residents. It is illustrated with agricultural, tourist and domestic artefacts, costume, paintings and fossils, a large collection of local books, photographs and maps.

Dapdune Wharf
Navigations Office & Dapdune Wharf, Wharf Road, Guildford, GU1 4RR tel: 01483 561389
An old working wharf on the River Wey, with a series of interactive exhibits and displays allowing the discovery of the fascinating story of Surrey's secret waterway, one of the first British rivers to be made navigable.

Museum of Farnham
Willmer House, 38 West Street, Farnham, Surrey, GU9 7DX
tel: 01252 715094
A local history museum housed in a Grade I listed town house built in 1718. The museum features innovative displays relating to the history of Farnham and surrounding villages.

Godalming Museum
109a High Street, Godalming, Surrey GU7 1AQ
tel: 01483 426510
Godalming Museum is situated in a medieval building and it presents the history of Godalming and surrounding villages through displays and trails. Local initiatives active in the field of sustainability and community building are engaged to look at past ways of life and current ideas and hopes for a sustainable way of living.

Guildford House Gallery
155 High Street, Guildford, Surrey GU1 3AJ
Guildford House Gallery is a Grade II listed building from 1660

with many original features. It offers a mixed programme of temporary exhibitions.

Guildford Museum

Castle Arch, Quarry Street, Guildford, Surrey, GU1 3SX
tel: 01483 444750
Guildford Museum offers the largest collection of archaeology, local history and needlework in Surrey. Displays include local characters such as Lewis Carroll and Gertrude Jekyll. It is housed in a beautiful 17th century building next to the castle grounds. The archaeology shows life in Surrey from prehistoric times to the Middle Ages and crafts and industries, together with sections on Lewis Carroll and Gertrude Jekyll.

Haslemere Educational Museum

78 High Street, Haslemere, Surrey, GU27 2LA tel: 01428 642112
Set in beautiful gardens, Haslemere Museum is known colloquially as the "miniature British Museum covering stunning geology, natural history and human history collections. These include a significant Peasant Art collection, Geikie watercolours and their own Egyptian mummy.

Hatchlands Park

East Clandon, Guildford, Surrey, GU4 7RT tel: 01483 222482
Hatchlands is one of the largest country estates surrounding Greater London. It is an historic house, containing a magnificent collection of musical instruments. Hatchlands Park was built in the 1750s for Admiral Edward Boscawen. On display is the Cobbe Collection, Europe's largest collection of keyboard instruments associated with famous composers including Bach, Chopin and Elgar. Over 400 acres of parkland provide many marked walks.

Holmesdale Natural History Museum

14 Croydon Rd, Reigate, Surrey, RH2 0PG, tel: 01737 247092
The Holmesdale Natural History Museum has extensive collections of the natural history. It include insects, stuffed birds, herbarium specimens, geological specimens, local history and archaeological collections and promotes the study of natural history, local history, archaeology and geology in the area of Reigate.

Leatherhead Museum

Hampton Cottage, 64 Church Street, Leatherhead, Surrey, KT22 8DP tel: 01372 374093
Housed in a 17th century timber-framed listed building, Leatherhead Museum offers an interesting collection of local memorabilia and archaeological artefacts from excavations in the area.

Oakhurst Cottage

Hambledon, near Godalming, Surrey, GU8 4HF
tel: 01483 208477
Oakhurst Cottage shows how life used to be lived in the past in rural Surrey. It is a restored and furnished simple labourer's dwelling, containing artefacts reflecting four centuries of continual occupation. There is also a delightful cottage garden.

Polesden Lacey

Great Bookham, near Dorking, Surrey, RH5 6BD
tel: 01372 452048
A Regency villa bought by an Edwardian hostess in 1906. This elegant country house displays world-class collections of art and furniture. The long grass terrace walk dates from 1671 and was extended by the playwright Sheridan, who lived here from 1797-1816. The Edwardian garden has a series of walled and hedged enclosures with roses and herbaceous planting.

Reigate Priory Museum

Riegate, Priory School, Reigate Priory, Bell Street, Reigate, Surrey RH2 7RL tel: 01737 222550
Reigate Priory is a Grade I listed building set in 65 acres of open parkland with a pond, woodland and playing fields. It is home to Reigate Priory Museum and Reigate Priory School. Artefacts

concerning local history and social history are displayed there. Collections of domestic items, archaeology, artwork and pictures all aid in giving an insight into past times in the local area.

Royal Earlswood Museum

The Belfry Centre, Redhill RH1 1ST tel: 01737 216238
Small collection of exhibits illustrating the history and development of Earlswood Asylum. There is also a collection of the works of its most famed resident James Henry Pullen the 'idiot genius'.

Rural Life Centre

Reeds Row, Tilford, Farnham, Surrey, GU10 2DL
tel: 01252 795571
Rural life and social history from 1800 - 1960 is shown through buildings and exhibitions.

Shalford Mill

Shalford, near Guildford, GU4 8BS tel: 01483 561389
Shalford Mill is a wonderful hidden gem; it sits on the Tillingbourne, in the quiet backwater of Shalford. The National Trust runs regular guided tours of this early 18th-century watermill. The building has remained almost unaltered since ceasing operations in 1914.

Shere Museum

Gomshall Lane, Shere, Surrey, GU5 9HE
tel: 01483 202769/203245
Situated in the picturesque village of Shere, the many displays include objects of daily life – tools, toys, domestic items – mainly from Victorian times to the 1950s, as well as Shere's famous connections with film and photography. There is also extensive information, including the local history society archive.

The Spike

Warren Road, Guildford, GU1 3JH tel: 01483 569944
The Guildford Union Workhouse as it was in 1906. Visible for miles, a place for homeless and poor of the 19th and 20th centuries. This most innovative on-going heritage project, the Vagrants and Casual Ward of the Guildford Union Workhouse tells a very interesting story of the workhouse inmates and conditions they lived in.

Surrey Infantry Museum

Clandon Park, West Clandon, Guildford, Surrey GU4 7RQ
tel: 01483 223419
Set in Clandon Park House, the museum tells the story of Surrey's two infantry regiments from 1661 until the present day through medals, uniforms, artefacts and interactive displays.

Surrey Police Museum

Mount Browne, Sandy Lane, Guildford, Surrey, GU3 1HG
tel: 01483 482155
A museum portraying the history of the force was opened at Mount Brown, the Surrey Constabulary's headquarters in Guildford. Displays include reconstructions of a gaol cell and a crime scene as well as artefacts and touch-screen technology, all tracing the history of the force up to the present day

The Watts Gallery

Down Lane, Compton, Nr Guildford, Surrey, GU3 1DQ
tel: 01483 810235
A gallery devoted to the symbolist artist, G.W. Watts, first opened to the public on 1 April 1904. The collection in the gallery consists of paintings, drawings, prints and sculpture that were owned by Watts; all works were given by him to the nation. The gallery is an early example of an Arts and Crafts building.

Winkworth Arboretum

Hascombe Road, Godalming, GU8 4AD tel: 01483 208477
Winkworth Arboretum was founded by Dr Wilfrid Fox in 1937 and is set in some 46 hectares. Whilst it is well known for its autumn colours it is a pleasant place to visit any time of the year. It has an award-winning collection of over 1000 different shrubs and trees.

Famous People Associated with Surrey Hills

Abbott, George – born in 1562 in Guildford, died 1633, Archbishop of Canterbury. Studied and taught at Balliol College, Oxford. Master of University College in 1597, Dean of Winchester in 1600, archbishop of Canterbury from 1611.

Austen, Jane – born in 1775, died in 1817. English novelist, one of the most widely read writers, author of romantic fiction books: *Sense and Sensibility, Pride and prejudice, Emma, Northanger Abbey, Persuasion.*

Barrie, James – born 1860, died 1937, baronet, member of the Order of Merit, Scottish dramatist, best remembered as the author of *Peter Pan.*

Beecham, Thomas – born 1879, died 1961, British conductor, founder of several orchestras, amongst them, the Royal Philharmonic Orchestra.

Boscawen, Edward – born 1711, died 1761, an admiral in the Royal Navy, member of Parliament, Lord Commissioner of the Admiralty, member of the Privy Council.

Brodie, Benjamin – born 1783, died 1862, physiologist and surgeon. Fellow of the Royal Society from 1810, contributing papers to the Medical and Chirurgical Society, sergeant-surgeon to William IV and Queen Victoria, member of French Institute, president of the Royal Society and General Medical Council.

Carroll, Lewis – born 1832, died 1898, mathematician, logician, Anglican deacon, photographer, author of *Alice's Adventures in Wonderland* and *Through the Looking Glass.*

Chambers, William – born 1723, died 1796, Scottish architect, designed Somerset House and Kew Pagoda.

Christie, Agatha – born 1890, died 1976. Dame of the British Empire, writer and author of many books, including *Death on the Nile* and *Murder on the Orient Express.*

Cobbett, William – born 1763 in Farnham, died 1835, English journalist and pamphleteer. Best known for his book *Rural Rides.*

Colman, Jeremiah – born 1859, died 1942, industrialist, developed Colman's Mustard, Chairman of Commercial Union, High Sheriff of Surrey, owner of Gatton Park.

Conrad, Joseph – born 1857 as Józef Korzeniowski, died 1924, Polish writer who became a British national. He wrote in English and was viewed as a precursor of modernist literature. Regarded as one of the greatest novelist in English, works include *Lord Jim, Nostromo, The Duel, The Secret Agent.*

Cubitt, Thomas – born 1788, died 1855, master builder, designed London Institution in Finsbury Circus, buildings in Belgravia, Denbies Estate in Dorking, Eaton Square and responsible for the east wing of Buckingham Palace.

Darke, Harold – born 1888, died 1976, composer and organist, director of Music at King's College in Cambridge, best known for his music for Christina Rossetti's "In the Bleak Midwinter" considered the greatest Christmas Carol.

Defoe, Daniel – born 1660, died 1731, writer, journalist and spy, famous for his novel *Robinson Crusoe.* He wrote over 500 books, pamphlets and journals.

Delius, Frederick – born 1862, died 1934, composer.

Doyle, Arthur Conan – born 1859, died 1930, writer, most noted for "Sherlock Holmes".

Drummond, Henry – born 1786, died 1860, politician, banker, Member of Parliament, writer, founder of the Catholic Apostolic or Irvingite Church, owner of Albury Park.

Elliot, George – born 1819 as Mary Ann Evans, died 1880, known by her male pen name, novelist, journalist and translator. Author of seven novels, including *Daniel Deronda, The Mill on the Floss*.

Evelyn, John – born in 1620, died in 1706, writer, gardener, diarist.

Falkner, Harold – born in 1875, died in 1963, architect and designer, leading exponent of Arts & Crafts in architectural work in West Surrey.

Hemar, Marian – born in 1901, died in 1972. Polish poet, playwright, songwriter and comedy writer. Settled in England in 1941. Died and buried in Coldharbour.

Hill, Octavia – born in 1838, died in 1912, social reformer, campaigning for social housing, against development of suburban woodlands, founder of the National Trust.

Hitchcock, Alfred – born in 1899, died in 1980, film director and producer, best known for his psychological thrillers. His best known films: *The 39 steps, Vertigo, Psycho, The Birds* and *Frenzy*.

Howard, Leslie – born in 1893, died in 1943, stage and film actor. Some of his best known roles are in *Gone with the Wind, Scarlet Pimpernel, Pygmalion, The first of the few*.

Jekyll, Gertrude – born in 1843, died in 1932. Garden designer, writer, horticulturalist and artist. She designed over 400 gardens.

Langton, Stephen – born in 1150, died in 1228, Archbishop of Canterbury.

Lovelace, Ada – born in 1815, died in 1852, daughter of Lord Byron, mathematician and writer, famous for her notes on Analytical Engine which are recognised as the first algorithm for machine processing, hence considered the world's first computer programmer.

Lutyens, Edwin – born in 1869, died in 1944, architect and designer modernising traditional style in English country houses. His prolific career encompassed numbers of country houses, fine commercial buildings, monuments and most famously, the Viceroy's House, the centrepiece of New Delhi.

Maufe, Edward – born in 1883, died in 1974, architect and designer. Designed over 50 buildings, best known for Guildford Cathedral.

Nightingale, Florence – born in 1820, died in 1910, social reformer and founder of modern nursing. She laid the foundation for professional nursing, established a nursing school at St. Thomas' Hospital in London, and campaigned to improve healthcare and participation of women at work.

Oliver, Laurence – born in 1907, died in 1989, actor, director and producer. Starred on stage and in many films including *Othello, Twelfth Night, Marathon Man, Rebecca* and *A Bridge too Far*.

Pugin, August – born in 1812, died in 1852, architect, designer. Responsible for the interior design of Palace of Westminster and many churches in England.

Reed, Oliver – born in 1938, died in 1999, actor. Best known for roles in *Oliver, The Three Musketeers, Lion of the Desert* and *Gladiator*.

Tennyson, Alfred – born in 1809, died in 1892, poet, author of *Break, break, break, The Charge of the Light Brigade, Idylls of the King.*

Thomas, Inigo – born in 1865, died in 1950, garden designer and artist.

Tyndall, John – born in 1820, died in 1893, physicist, famous for his discoveries of atmosphere processes.

Williams, Ralph Vaughan – born in 1872, died in 1958, composer of symphonies, choral music, chamber music and film scores, collector of English folk music.

Webb, Philip – born in 1831, died in 1915, architect. Called the Father of Arts and Crafts Architecture. Designed many houses: Red House at Bexleyheath, Standen House and many more.

Woodyer, Henry – born in 1816, died in 1896, architect, designed St Martin's church in Dorking.

View from Leith Hill.